THE ROAD TO LONDON BRIDGE

THE ROAD TO LONDON BRIDGE

Steve Gallant

SEVEN DIALS

First published in Great Britain in 2023 by Seven Dials,
an imprint of The Orion Publishing Group Ltd
Carmelite House, 50 Victoria Embankment
London EC4Y 0DZ

An Hachette UK Company

1 3 5 7 9 10 8 6 4 2

A CIP catalogue record for this book is
available from the British Library.

ISBN (Paperback) 978 1 3996 0485 7
ISBN (Audiobook) 978 1 3996 0487 1
ISBN (eBook) 978 1 3996 0486 4

Typeset by Born Group
Printed and bound in Great Britain by Clays Ltd, Elcograf S.p.A.

www.orionbooks.co.uk

This book is a story of redemption. It is not intended in any way to endorse or promote the use of violence. Reference to criminal activity is included only for context, as part of the story, both for educational purposes and in the public interest. The crime for which the author was convicted is not the focus nor the essence of the book. Recollections of certain events may vary, but the author recounts matters to the best of his knowledge and belief and with no intention to cause distress to any other person.

CONTENTS

PROLOGUE:

London Bridge

It was my first day out of prison in fourteen and a half years.

As if to show me what I'd been missing all this time, the sky was a fierce blue and the sun shone brightly across London. The city was buzzing. People moved briskly about their day, just as I once had, taking for granted a fundamental right it's easy to forget we even have – until it is taken away.

I had Learning Together, a Cambridge University initiative that offers education opportunities for prisoners, to thank for my new-found, albeit temporary freedom. I had been invited to a conference to celebrate their five-year anniversary at Fishmongers' Hall in London Bridge. And while my 'plus one' was my escorting officer Adam, it was still an incredible feeling to be outside and in the real world. It was a privilege to see the people who had helped me so enormously during the later stages of my sentence outside of the prison setting.

So the last thing I expected, just a matter of hours later, was to find myself holding, of all things, a narwhal tusk as a makeshift weapon and going toe to toe with a knife-wielding terrorist wearing an explosive belt. After fourteen and a half years in prison and having taken a vow to renounce violence, I would never have believed that I'd be forced to resort to using it on my first day out.

The high-pitched screams had first got our attention while we were in the banqueting hall upstairs at

Fishmongers' Hall. I was given orders by Adam to stay put while he went off to investigate. But when the screams persisted and confusion and concern spread like wildfire around the room, I had to go down and find out what was going on.

It was chaos. Two young women lay on the floor at the bottom of the stairs. Adam was kneeling over one of them, trying desperately to stem the heavy flow of blood from her neck. The other lay in a pool of her own blood. People were hiding or running scared. Screams echoed around the illustrious surroundings.

So here I was, face to face with Usman Khan, another guest of the Learning Together event, but one who had so cruelly betrayed the trust shown in him. He had a razor-sharp, eight-inch blade taped to each wrist and an explosive vest around his body; I had a narwhal tusk, one of a pair that I'd seen earlier in the day attached to the wall as part of a display. I didn't hesitate. My plan was to slow him down or stop him by any means possible. He'd already demonstrated the lengths to which he was prepared to go. I tried to stay on my toes, light-footed, while wielding the narwhal tusk like a lance in a jousting match.

Usman came first, swinging his knives towards me, but I took advantage of my extra reach to thrust the tusk straight into his chest. I hit him hard – but it seemed to have little effect. We both backed off. I was surprised the blow hadn't been more effective, but there was no time to dwell on it as we moved back and forth, jostling for a better striking position. I struck out, missing by a whisker . . . His knives came close . . . and then, *Crunch!* I managed to hit him hard across the shoulder, snapping the narwhal tusk in the process. I backed off quickly.

When Usman burst out of the door of Fishmongers' Hall onto the street, I went after him. It was bright out there. The streets were busy, the traffic on the far side of the road almost at a standstill. Usman was heading towards London Bridge. I could see several women walking directly towards him, oblivious.

'Get back!' I shouted, while waving my arms to draw their attention. 'It's a terrorist!'

Alerted to the danger, they turned and swiftly backed away. Other guests followed me out of Fishmongers' Hall and began shouting too.

As I reached the pavement at the bottom of the stone steps outside Fishmongers' Hall, Usman turned to face me. I struck him again with the broken narwhal tusk but somehow he managed to grab it and rip it from my hands. I backed off towards the steps as he threw it at me.

I felt a cold sensation on my arm. It was the spray from a fire extinguisher, fired haphazardly towards Usman by another pursuer. Usman turned and suddenly began running towards the bridge. Another man carrying the other narwhal tusk joined the chase and raced ahead of me. I followed suit.

It felt like time had slowed down. My blood was loaded with adrenaline, enhancing my reaction time.

As we reached Usman on London Bridge, he turned to face us again. He lunged and began swinging his knives towards one of the pursuers.

Just grab him, I told myself. *Take him to the ground.* I made a lunge for his jacket with both hands and we went down.

'Grab his hands!' I shouted to the other two.

The chap with the narwhal tusk jumped in to take hold of Usman while passers-by began helping too. Some people jumped out of their cars to assist us.

One of the guests from Fishmongers' Hall came running up. 'Give him a kicking!' he screamed.

'No! Don't hit him!' I shouted back. We had to retain control. He still held his knives and could detonate his explosives. Then, somehow, Usman managed to get back to his feet. In the confusion that followed it was impossible to tell who had control, but then a gap opened for a moment, offering me an unobstructed view of his face. I punched him hard in the jaw. *Crack!* And another: *Crack!* This time, when he went down under us all, he remained there.

As I walked away from Usman Khan after the armed police had arrived and his body had been filled with bullets, a whirlwind of thoughts went round my head, my adrenaline beginning to come down from its intoxicating peak. *Did that really just happen?*

My previous act of violence had cost someone their life, shattered many others in the process and landed me a murder conviction in 2005, a life sentence with a minimum tariff of 17 years.

Shocked and confused, yet struck by a sudden moment of clarity, I turned to the chap with the narwhal tusk and said, 'That was my first act of violence in fourteen and a half years.'

I'd broken my vow.

PART I

The Start of the Road

CHAPTER I

City of Culture

The detectives were in no doubt. Whoever attacked Ms Ives had intended to kill her. She had no recollection of the incident but the pathologist who examined her injuries was able to establish that she had been forcefully struck to the ground and repeatedly stamped on until every bone in her face was broken, including her eye sockets. After beating her face to a pulp, her attacker had then picked her up like a rag doll and thrown her into a skip, leaving her to her fate. If it were not for her discovery by a man foraging for scrap metal on that quiet Sunday morning, Ms Ives, who by then had spent around ten hours under the cold November rain, would have been dead. Her body temperature was just 25 degrees, half a degree from death.

Like most big cities, Hull has its fair share of violent incidents, but there were some unusual features about this one. The woman they'd discovered at the rear of Staples Superstore in the city centre in 2002 was a 63-year-old bingo-loving pensioner who would pay occasional visits to Hull's red-light district. And the person arrested for attempting to kill her was employed as a fireman, stationed a few blocks away. It was big news at the time. I was working on a building site near Hull's KC stadium and I recall chatting with my colleagues about the alleged perpetrator, someone we sort of knew. But it was the kind of story that would gradually have dissipated from the city's consciousness if it had not been for the events that followed. Sitting on a pile of bricks while resting over lunch, I couldn't possibly have imagined how the story of that woman's ordeal would go on to resurface throughout my life.

A city-village that rests on the north side of the River Humber in East Yorkshire, Hull is isolated from other major cities, a feature that led to the development of a rather quirky but insular culture. Bred mostly on blue-collar industries and working-class ideals, of the type that expect you to work hard for a living but leave you equally uninspired by lack of promotion prospects, its people are a tough-minded bunch, yet few visitors leave the city without noting its friendliness.

With its docks and ferry port visible at the mouth of the River Humber, Hull also offers access to the European continent and its treasures. But the ideological currents that flow inwards through this river have never really impressed Hull's working class. When the fishing industry collapsed, an event that was attributed to Britain's flirtation with the European Union and the Icelandic Cod Wars, the damage it caused to Hull's economy left deep scars in the psychology of its people. Over the years, Hull did recover lost ground, but not enough to insulate it from the 2008 financial crash, which exposed its industrial limitations and opened up opportunities to immigrants willing to trade their skills at a more competitive rate. Again, 'because of Europe!' the people of Hull were out of pocket. So when a Conservative referendum in 2016 brought the opportunity to depart the largest trading block in the world and set sail in a different direction, Hull voted overwhelmingly to leave.

The slump in Hull's economy was just as likely to do with domestic politics and the advance of globalisation, but that's how modern political campaigns appear to operate: someone spreads a myth and it festers, until enough people rush outside with a pitchfork and someone gets it.

I was born in 1977 in Hull and had lived there all my life. Although my father left the family home when I was three years old, my older brother and I would still spend time with him, at his flat. A good-natured and calm man, 'no violence' was his mantra. But he did like practical jokes. Once, when I was around five years old, he bought us an Atari games console.

'Boys, I'm nipping t' shops. If owt goes wrong with the TV screen, get out the house quick as you can,' he warned us. 'It's very dangerous and could explode!'

After Dad popped out, we shrugged our shoulders and continued playing. Around five minutes later, the TV screen suddenly went fuzzy. With Dad's words ringing in our ears, we tried to leave the flat but the living-room door was locked. While keeping a desperate eye on the TV, we pulled at the handle until we worked ourselves into a frenzy, screaming in terror. Of course, Dad was standing behind the door, laughing his head off.

The 1980s were a pretty tough period for my mother to be raising us. We lived on council estates in East Hull, a part of the country where the effects of a recession lingered a little longer than elsewhere and, in my neighbourhood, packs of feral dogs invaded the playground to chase the kids. I recall it vividly, along with the social deprivation. Unhappy with life on Bransholme estate, one of Europe's largest, my mother moved us on to Longhill estate and to a different school. But after I was sent home for kicking someone in my new playground, it was clear that self-discipline was not going to be one of my fortes. Incapable of gaining the approval of my schoolteachers, I naturally drifted towards like-minded kids.

Violence and aggression were always present throughout my youth. As a child, I was quite skinny and weak, which left me vulnerable to assault from other kids, even friends. And if I wasn't the target of domestic violence from my stepfather, a rugby player who grew way too fond of knocking the shit out of me for minor house-rule infringements, there was often an older bully waiting on the pavement to give me a slap or force me to say the Lord's Prayer backwards. Resilience being the gift of every child, I shrugged it off. But the conditioning had begun.

My only respite was when my grandmother would take us on adventures to the Lake District or the countryside where she lived. She was a storyteller, ghosts and war being her usual subjects. And, as far as I was concerned, she had mystical powers.

'Read my tea leaves,' I would pester.

'Hmm, let's see,' she would say, glancing into the bottom of my cup to read my fortune.

She had lived through the German bombing raids across Hull during the Second World War, which began on her fourteenth birthday, and had known hardship as a child, so she tried to create for us kids what she had lacked in her own childhood. She understood more than anyone that a certain type of wisdom could only be attained through overcoming adversity. One such arduous adventure my grandma took us on saw me standing on the summit of Harrison Stickle, a 736-metre peak in the Lake District which we climbed when I was seven. The experience of gazing at the valley below and reflecting on the journey instilled in me a profound appreciation for the power of patience and perseverance in the face of tough challenges.

But though these lessons remained in the depths of my mind, they were vastly overshadowed by the culture that had already seeped into my bones. I received my first visit from the police when I was ten years old. And by the age of seventeen, during which time I'd acquired four more siblings, I'd finalised my education at a school for naughty kids, left with no qualifications and had racked up a large number of convictions for fighting and petty offences, culminating in an eight-month prison sentence. There was nothing too serious among those crimes, but they were enough to hinder my job prospects and prevent me from joining the army.

My only real discipline came from rugby. Having two top-flight teams, Hull KR and Hull FC, meant rugby league was the main choice of sport for kids across Hull. But those rugby pitches could be unforgiving places. Dirty play was customary and, in a region exposed to North Sea winds, the grass could freeze over like glass during the winter months. Still, you were expected to shrug it off, so we did, with a smile. If Hull's culture encompasses values like resilience, solidarity and the audacity to be different, it's partly because of the wet and muddy rugby pitches scattered throughout its landscape.

Of course, Hull does have a softer side to it – a history of producing actors, writers and artistic movements, and it was the UK City of Culture in 2017. A phrase or two from one of Hull's famous poets was never going to be part of my vernacular, however. When you spend your school days wondering where the next punch is coming from, the last thing that's going to help is a quote from Philip Larkin.

CHAPTER 2

Growing Up

'What you done?' I asked Danny as he sat there on a beach towel, sulking while the other kids paddled in the sea.

'Nowt,' he replied with his arms folded, scowling at the teacher.

This was the first conversation I remember having with Danny. On a school trip to Hornsea, we'd each been ordered to go and sit away from our classmates for misbehaving. We were seven years old and it was the beginning of a long relationship that would end in disaster.

Fast forward to 1992 and Danny and I were still up for mischief, but it was the bars and nightclubs of Hull that were our playground now. House music had taken off in the city and some of the buildings and warehouses left over from Hull's dock industry made ideal bars and clubs. Underaged and impressionable when Danny and I first discovered that world, we seamlessly picked up the habits of the town hard cases who had become our idols: speed, ecstasy, fighting.

Signing on and selling party drugs was never going to sustain such a lifestyle, so by the age of nineteen I began working. My group of friends had also begun to develop a reputation and Danny had become its natural leader. At six-foot-two, aggressive and with an air of arrogance, he was an obvious choice.

Back in East Hull, where territorial boundaries were more defined, the local pubs could be equally rough. One in particular was The Viking. To the casual observer, it was a dingy local that you wouldn't be seen dead in. Scarfed in barbed wire and monitored by CCTV, it certainly looked the part. But it was the epicentre of our universe, a second home from where we launched our escapades into other territories and to which we retired to lick our wounds.

But not everyone agreed to our presence. Struggling to turn a profit at one time, the brewery settled on a new landlord who had a reputation for dealing with 'trouble-makers'. He began his tenure by banning me and my friends from the pub. Returning later that evening, Danny confronted the landlord in the crowded bar. With music blaring and the locals watching in anticipation, the landlord squared up to Danny with his large frame.

'You letting me in or what?' Danny demanded.

Out of nowhere, the landlord launched a heavy right hand that sent Danny flying across the room and crashing to the floor. This landlord was not up for compromise. Twenty seconds later, he was at the back of the pub trying to fend off ten lads with a speaker stand while others trashed the bar. Not long after, The Viking reopened with a new landlord.

It wasn't always like that. We mostly worked for a living and tried to enjoy ourselves with minimal hassle. It was just accepted that if trouble arose, you stuck together. And if you were ever arrested or hospitalised, you kept your mouth shut. That's how things remained, until, at the age of twenty-three, I decided to settle down – or at least, I tried.

It was her legs, while she ran for the bus one day, that first caught my eye. With long, dark curly hair, brown eyes and a beautiful smile, she was perfect. I'd seen her around – she was a waitress at a bar in the town centre. We had a few friends in common, some social overlap, but we'd never really spoken more than a few words to each other before.

We bumped into each other on the street one afternoon and hit it off straight away. Her name was Jayne.

'I've got a fiver in my pocket,' she said. 'Wanna pop into The Viking for half?'

This was back in the days when a fiver would buy you three or four drinks.

'Yeah, why not,' I responded.

It was a whirlwind romance and it didn't take long before we moved in together, in a flat on our estate, an arrangement that was unworkable unless I found a job and kept it. *Nothing like a good kick up the arse,* I thought. It was one that brought some stability to my life and culminated in me working as a gas engineer.

Jayne and I settled into a relationship but, despite her affection and the stability of a comfortable home, old habits die hard.

'I'm going home. You coming or what?' she would ask while holding the door open at a friend's house after a night out.

'Just one more, Jayne,' I'd respond, as Danny and my friends lay sprawled out on the floor.

'It's four o'clock in the morning, Steve!'

Her friends would tell me I didn't know how lucky I was to have her. But I did. She was devoted to me and faithful to the core. I just couldn't settle. By the spring of 2005, we'd been together over five years but our relationship was being tested by my lifestyle. It was an odd choice, occupying the floor of my mother's spare bedroom, rather than sharing a double bed with my partner. But that was me, very self-destructive.

CHAPTER 3

Lighting the Fuse

The clock had just gone midnight, on Saturday 16 April 2005, when two men and a woman climbed out of a car and quickly made their way towards a block of flats. As they approached the communal doorway, one of the men and the woman each began to cover their faces with a pair of tights, and the other man covered his with a balaclava. Once inside, they pulled out their weapons. For the man wearing the balaclava, this was a hammer. They meant business and their target was the occupant of 200 Atlantic Road. On reaching the front door of the flat, they could hear music and laughter coming from inside. Eager to go, the person holding the hammer assumed the lead position.

Inside the flat, Jayne was enjoying a few drinks with her friends, having not long returned from the local pub. She heard a knock at the door and, expecting more friends to arrive, hurried to see who was there. As she opened the door, Jayne saw the masked individuals bunched in the hallway. For a second, she thought someone was messing around, until she saw a white flash. She had been struck on the forehead with a hammer. Stunned from the blow, she fell backwards into the kitchen while the masked assailants pushed past her to enter the living room.

Jayne tried to compose herself as blood began to trickle down her forehead and onto the palm of her hand. Screams were now coming from the living room. Dazed and in shock, but fearing for her friends, Jayne plucked up the courage to go and see what was happening. As she entered, she saw Oliver, one of her guests, lying on the floor. Blood covered his face. He had approached the living-room door expecting to greet new arrivals but been struck with a blow to the head. By now, the three assailants were shouting, 'Where's the five grand? Where's the drugs?' while continuing to hit and threaten people.

Another friend of Jayne's was struck over the head, opening up a deep gash. At one point, everyone was told to empty their pockets and hand over their possessions. Weapons were held to their faces while demands were made to reveal the whereabouts of the 'scousers'. One of the attackers tried setting someone alight while another smashed the stereo to pieces.

Jayne pleaded with the aggressors: 'What are you doing? Who are you?' But her pleas were met with further threats of violence.

Oliver managed to crawl to a chair but again he was beaten over the head. To those huddled in the corner of the living room, it was clear who was in charge: the man wearing the balaclava. With the lights on, Jayne thought she recognised him.

'Are you Bam Bam?' she asked.

'No,' he replied. 'Shut up!'

After what seemed like an eternity of torment, the man wearing the balaclava gave the order to his accomplices: 'Take whatever you want. Come on, we're off.'

The gang pocketed what they could. Before leaving, the man in charge turned to Jayne one last time: 'You have one week to get out, or I'll kill you.'

★

I was out drinking that night with my mates when I received a phone call saying Jayne had been attacked. I headed straight over.

By the time I arrived, the police had cordoned off the entrance and paramedics were inside the flat tending to the injured. Jayne and her friends were clearly in shock. Their faces were blank – but there was also a sense of relief that the ordeal was over.

My worry abated slightly when I realised Jayne was OK – to an extent. But my feelings swiftly turned to anger and confusion. *Who would do such a thing?*

And then, of course, there was another question: *Why?*

Jayne and I weren't drug dealers; we both worked for a living. Why would anyone be looking for that kind of money or for drugs in our home? Was it a case of mistaken identity – they'd targeted the wrong flat? Or was something else at play here?

The man Jayne thought she'd recognised was Craig Peterson, a guy from a nearby council estate known locally as 'Bam Bam'. While I'd been staying at my mother's, Craig had been visiting a girl who'd recently moved into the flat next door to Jayne. Jayne had formed a cordial relationship with her new neighbour, or so she'd thought. But after believing she'd recognised Craig, she suspected her music may have been the cause of the attack. It sounded dubious, but Craig had form.

Like many living in Hull during that time, I was aware of his reputation and recent encounters with the law. We'd also gone to the same senior school but we'd never spoken to each other. He was slightly older than me and

I found him intimidating, so I kept my distance. But that's only my recollection. He was said to have a good side to his nature and seemed popular with some associates on his estate. He'd also once served in the armed forces and later joined the fire brigade, an occupation in which he undoubtedly placed himself at great risk to help others.

But it was while Craig was working as a fireman that he had been arrested and tried for the attempted murder of Carol Ives, the 63-year-old lady who was discovered in a skip in Hull town centre, three years earlier. Craig was eventually acquitted for that crime but immediately afterwards he was sentenced to two years for punching unconscious and breaking the jaw of 43-year-old Rosalina Cappell, who had tried to call the police while Craig was attacking his elderly father. Due to his conviction and the extensive coverage of his trial in the *Hull Daily Mail*, as well as a statement from Humberside Police stating they weren't looking for anyone else in relation to the attempted murder of Carol Ives, many in the city believed Craig had narrowly escaped a far heavier sentence, a notion reinforced by Detective Superintendent Paul Davison when he warned the public that Craig Peterson was 'a very violent and dangerous man'.

Despite all this, I still believed Jayne was mistaken about his possible involvement. The attack was too excessive for a bit of music and the girl next door hadn't complained. On the face of it, it looked like a gang of violent drug addicts had got the wrong address. Jayne's suspicions fell on deaf ears – mine, to be precise. I just couldn't see it. The name of Jacob Clifton came up – a crackhead who'd also been recognised under the tights he'd worn to conceal his identity – and I was confident this seemed the more likely explanation.

My feelings when I arrived on the scene, once I knew Jayne would be OK, had been anger. I was initially angry at myself: why wasn't I there to protect Jayne? I felt guilty. If I'd been there would this have happened at all? There's no way I would have just stood by while someone hit my girlfriend over the head with a hammer. But the more I thought about it, the more I realised that if I'd been there I might have ended up escalating things further, perhaps even risking my own life. The perpetrators had been armed and were clearly dangerous, and didn't care who they hit, so who knows how things might have ended. Despite my initial instincts, it might have been for the best that I wasn't there. Though that didn't make me any less determined to get to the bottom of what had happened here.

The next day, Jayne and I returned to the flat to clean up the mess. By chance, Craig was also heading towards the same block of flats with his partner. To Jayne's surprise, I waited for them to reach us and asked if they had seen anything the previous night.

'I heard noises,' replied his partner, 'but I didn't dare look outside.'

'I arrived later but the police on the door wouldn't let me in,' Craig said. 'If you have any more trouble, just give me a shout.'

'Nice one, mate,' I replied, before walking off.

As soon as the door shut behind us in the flat, Jayne's eyes widened. 'It was him,' she said. Seeing him in the flesh reaffirmed her belief that he was responsible.

I shook my head. 'It's not him,' I replied. His calm response had made me doubt her even more.

I took some pictures of the damage before comforting Jayne. She was still shaking, the claw-hammer mark on her forehead testament to the ordeal she and her friends had endured. Whoever had carried out that act, I thought to myself, was cowardly and cruel. Jayne and her friends were hard-working, law-abiding people. And this was my home. I could feel the anger beginning to rise through me. I told her I would find who'd done it. It was mostly wishful thinking, my way of trying to placate my sense of guilt over my absence, but Jayne was concerned.

'Don't do anything, Steve,' she said categorically.

I gave her a hug.

Later that day, Jayne was interviewed by a police officer and given assurances that Craig would be arrested, as he was currently on bail for other offences and was being monitored under public protection arrangements. Although Jayne was offered police protection if charges were brought, she never returned to the flat again.

The next day, I was in The Sailors Arms with Jayne when a female associate of Craig's walked in. She pulled us to one side and lowered her voice as she began to speak. What she revealed ended my doubts about Craig's involvement. A friend of hers had been with Craig at another pub before the attack and she'd heard him mention Jayne's name and say, 'If she doesn't turn that music down, I'm gonna go in there and fucking sort her out.'

After hearing this, everything clicked. The only item that had been purposefully targeted in the flat was the sound system. And while the attackers had demanded drugs and money, not once did they make the effort to search the property. In any case, if they'd entered the flat purely to steal drugs and money, why would the man wearing the balaclava say to Jayne, 'You have one week to get out or I'll kill you!'

Ideally, this information should have been passed to the police but the person who told us this asked not to be identified for fear of reprisals. She had children. We had no choice but to respect that.

News travels fast and it wasn't long before our whole community was aware of who was the likely perpetrator of the aggravated burglary. Over the following days, more claims surfaced, one of them linking Craig to Jacob Clifton, the other suspect. Word on the street was that Craig had paid him and a woman £20 each to join him. And we later learned that, around thirty minutes before the attack on Jayne, Craig, in a sudden hurry, had got up and left his drinking associates after his partner had called him to complain about some music.

Although the allegations against Craig had not been proven in a court of law, in my mind he was responsible for the attack. And that meant if I saw him, there was a high chance my approach would be a touch different to our last encounter.

CHAPTER 4

One More Won't Hurt

It was a Sunday just like any other. After enjoying the weekend in the city centre bars and clubs, I spent the afternoon of 24 April 2005 in the local pubs with Danny and a group of friends, slowly coming round from a cocktail of drink and drugs while listening to tacky jukebox music. Nine days had passed since the aggravated burglary and, though we'd heard nothing from the police, I'd been warned that Craig was looking for me. I had to watch my back now, but as we never drank in the same pubs the chances of bumping into him again remained slim.

By around eight o'clock that evening, our group had dwindled, the last few of us heading to The Swiss Cottage pub. In the car park outside, a friend of mine was drunk and acting a nuisance with a CS canister, pretending to spray people in the face, so I took it off him before entering the pub. Danny and the others didn't last much longer, leaving me on my own, so I joined Tony, another friend.

'Fancy Sailors for last orders?' he asked.

I was about to go home. 'One more won't hurt,' I said.

Ten minutes later, we arrived at The Sailors Arms, the sound of karaoke playing loudly from within. As we entered the pub forecourt, I saw Rory, another friend of mine, in the doorway, looking agitated.

'Just been trying to call you,' he said, with his phone in hand. 'He's in there!'

My anger surged. 'What the fuck's he doing here?' I replied, bouncing up and down.

Tony disappeared into the pub and I looked through a side window. It was steamed up but I could see that the bar was crowded. The local football team had won their league. If I entered, it would be chaos. Full of alcohol and too blinded by my emotions to think of anything else but confronting Craig, I decided to wait by the side of the derelict bingo hall opposite the pub, where it was dark.

Craig had company, so Rory did the rounds and it wasn't long before Danny arrived in his van. My other mates, John, Frankie and Ted, showed up too. They entered the pub to keep an eye on Craig. My plan was to confront Craig on my own. It was between me and him.

I climbed into the passenger side of Danny's van. 'In case his mates jump in, watch my back,' I said – not that I needed to.

A hyped-up friend from inside the pub called my phone several times: 'Kick his fucking head in!'

Danny shouted across to Rory, 'Fucking get him out!'

At one point, Craig came rushing out of the pub with a broken pool cue in his hand, looking in all directions. He glanced towards the van, then, for some reason, went back inside.

Knowing that he was armed, I took the CS spray from my pocket, climbed out of the van and waited in a bush. Full of toxins, fuming over Jayne and encouraged by the presence of my mates, there was nothing to constrain my thoughts as my attention remained fixed on the pub doorway.

Suddenly, I saw Craig backing out of the pub while dragging someone by their feet and attacking them. Then, seconds later, a local called Jake intervened by punching

Craig in the face and sending him stumbling onto the pub forecourt.

At that moment, I shot out of the bush and raced towards him. At the same time, drinkers began spilling from the pub, following the commotion that had just erupted inside.

On reaching Craig, I slowed to a stop, just in front of him. He turned to face me, a hammer in his hand. I pointed the CS spray towards his face and pressed it. He started to run. I grabbed a beer bottle that someone had left on the pub wall and chased after him. As I caught up, I tried to hit him with the bottle. I missed and dropped it.

By now, we were running down the centre of the road and Craig was beginning to create some distance between us. Out of the corner of my eye, I noticed the lights from a vehicle. It was Danny. He shot past me and drove his van straight into Craig, smashing him to the ground and knocking him unconscious. I landed on top of Craig while he was sprawled out, face up, and began punching him. Within seconds, Danny was out the van and kicking Craig in the head. I caught a couple of glancing blows, so I stood up and joined in.

I became aware of a gathering crowd and people running towards us from the pub. My mates were among them, but others were friends of Craig, and young locals eager to catch a glimpse of the violence. Danny and I continued kicking Craig while those in the crowd shouted and jostled for position.

One girl had seen enough, however.

'You'll kill him!' she screamed.

'Fuck off!' I shouted back, before breaking off to retrieve Craig's hammer from the road near the back of the van. Craig's friends were lingering and I wanted to keep them at bay.

When I returned, Danny was still standing over Craig, giving him the odd boot and preventing the crowd from intervening. Pumped full of anger and adrenaline, I walked over to Craig and kicked his face several times. After I'd stopped, a collective silence fell on the scene. Enough was enough.

'You two, fuck off. Now!' Jake shouted.

Danny and I fled the scene in separate directions.

As my anger and adrenaline started to fade, I stopped. I couldn't help it. I made my way back to The Sailors Arms and hid in a bush not far from the scene. By now, an ambulance had arrived and a handful of onlookers obscured my view. Then Tony came strolling past with his head down. I called him over.

'It's bad, Ste,' said Tony, shaking his head. 'It's bad.'

'Is he dead?'

'I think so,' he replied.

My world suddenly shrank. I felt exposed and alone, as if my exact location was known and the police were heading straight towards it.

But he doesn't know he's dead for certain, I told myself.

'When the police question you, just tell 'em I left you before we reached The Sailors,' I instructed.

Tony nodded and walked on.

I pulled myself out of the bush and wandered down a dark cul-de-sac behind some nearby houses. I lit a cigarette. While taking a long, desperate drag from it, I looked up at the clear night sky. In the eerie quietness of that moment, I contemplated my entire existence, wondering what type of storm was coming. Out of the darkness, a dog suddenly jumped up at the fence next to me and began barking wildly, snapping me out of my daze.

I made my way to Rory's flat. To my relief, Rory insisted he wasn't dead. 'I swear down on me mam's life!' he said.

I made him repeat himself several times and questioned his logic, but he remained confident. I knew something wasn't right but it was reassuring to hear Rory say Craig wasn't dead. I breathed a sigh of relief and eventually fell asleep on Rory's sofa.

The next day, Rory and I woke to a radio announcement confirming Craig's death. To our disbelief, the news report also claimed that Craig had been killed with a hammer.

If I was meant to be hungover that morning, I certainly didn't feel it. With the emerging daylight flooding in through the windows and my conscience dripping with blood, I was acutely aware that nothing would ever be the same again. For the first time in my life, the lethal effects of unrestrained violence had been made clear to me. How had our objective seemed so justified and unmet, but then so grossly overreached within the blink of an eye? I noticed my hands shaking as I began to put on my clothes. It was like jumping into the abyss and then regretting it seconds later. 'Shit!'

But it was too late for thoughts like these. I needed to act — and act fast.

'I'll just say I wasn't there,' I told Rory, as if I'd just come up with a credible defence.

Rory could see the desperation on my face and simply agreed. He too must have been aware that over thirty witnesses had been present. After making a few frantic phone calls, we then set about disposing of the evidence and spent the rest of the morning trying to build an alibi.

This wasn't criminal values at play; it was self-preservation at full tilt. Driven by the fear of going to prison for an extremely long time, the impossibility of escape was buried under our surplus of adrenaline.

Under an overcast sky that perfectly reflected our mood, we spent the best part of the day criss-crossing from estate to estate, jumping over fences and weaving through back alleys.

'Just tell the police this . . .', 'Just tell them that . . .' we instructed friends and associates as we prepared to deny our culpability. We were clutching at paper straws but while the atmosphere remained sombre, the landscape had been kind and our community sympathetic. By mid-afternoon, our efforts were paying off. I'd found several people willing to support my alibi. Hope infused with delusion, the impossible had somehow lost its edge and suddenly my mind had something to hold on to.

As we were trudging through wasteland to our next destination, news came through that stopped us in our tracks: Danny had been arrested at his home that morning and was now in police custody.

In that very second, my objective altered. I turned to Rory. 'I'm handing myself in,' I said. 'We'll do it together.'

Danny and I were both responsible for Craig's death, but it was my grudge, which made it my duty to at least try and help him. I felt for Danny, knowing he was locked up in a police cell somewhere, but I was confident he was the best person to have by my side.

Everything slowed down again as we realised there was nothing more to run from. Rory and I were now openly walking the streets, coming to terms with the inescapable truth: I was going to prison for a very long time.

★

That same day, I travelled to Hull city centre with Rory to visit Steph Hutchinson, a solicitor who'd represented me before. After telling me that a manslaughter conviction was a likely outcome, Steph advised me to submit a brief statement rather than respond to any questions during the police interview.

The following day I drafted a statement outlining my movements on 24 April. I described most of my violence and my reason for confronting Craig. I'd also found out through the grapevine that Danny had admitted to seeing two people fighting on the floor and might have fallen onto them, so to help draw attention away from him, I inserted into my statement the words 'someone fell over us' and later maintained that I saw no one else make physical contact with Craig. To avoid any doubt, l later stated, 'I never meant it to happen the way it happened. I never meant to kill him.'

Steph called the police to let them know I was due to arrive, so, after saying goodbye to Rory, I set off on a slow walk to Hull's Central Police Station, just around the corner from Steph's office, through the foliage and birdlife of Queen's Gardens in the city's centre. It was a place I had cut through innumerable times in the twenty-eight years of my life but never before had I so intensely appreciated its existence.

While trying to absorb my last few moments of freedom, I passed by a bronze sculpture of a man sitting with his head bowed. He was encircled by metal bars protruding out of the ground. It was created by Jimmy Boyle, a reformed criminal who was once described as Scotland's most violent man. While serving time in one of Britain's most notorious prisons, he wrote a book called *A Sense of Freedom*. His sculpture looked how I felt.

Moments later, I reached the entrance of the police station, where two detectives were waiting outside to greet me. One of them smiled and held out his hand. I shook it, before being led inside.

PART II

The Vow

CHAPTER 5

HMP Hull

'All I did was hold an iron to the bitch's face!' complained the guy sitting next to me as I waited for my turn to get processed.

Eleven years had passed since my previous stint behind bars, at a young offender's institution and then in Hull prison for a few weeks, so my return to Hull prison on 29 April 2005 was pretty daunting. With its large sliding doors and turrets above, HMP Hull has one of those Victorian designs that immediately calls to mind the age of hangings. Fortunately, things had moved on since then. But if the combined smell of cigarette smoke, body odour and shit wasn't enough to alert me to the complexities that saturate prison environments, the chap next to me certainly did. With over a thousand prisoners held within its perimeter walls, HMP Hull was my reintroduction to the slow and laborious pace of prison of life, energised only by random flashes of violence or false alarms.

After looking through the names of former residents etched onto the holding-cell walls, I was stripped of my few possessions at the reception desk.

'Your crime?' asked the officer as he filled out a form with the words 'Remand' and 'Murder' written on it.

'I'll be pleading not guilty,' I replied.

It was at that point that I felt my status change. The way you're perceived and treated by others alters as your identity is officially taken from you and replaced with labels. I was no longer just Steve Gallant. I was a prisoner. A dangerous criminal. A killer, even. I didn't like it, but I understood.

With my new identity hung over my shoulders and a bed pack held tightly to my chest, I was introduced to my living quarters on the induction wing. Lying in my cell on that first night, listening to my neighbours offer each other free legal advice from their windows, I knew that if I was going to get through this in one piece, I would need to switch on.

Talk of our arrest was widespread and the other prisoners had been expecting us. To my surprise, I recognised many old faces from my adolescence. Now grown men, they had never quite managed to escape the never-ending cycle of crime and institutional failure.

As we paced around the prison exercise yard, Danny and I spoke in hushed tones. Danny was relieved to hear that I'd taken some of the heat off him. In return, he agreed to help me work towards a manslaughter conviction.

'If it fails,' I told him, 'I'll take the lot.'

We shook hands and gave each other a hug. At least we had each other.

Over the following week, we were both relocated to B Wing. I made the journey from the induction wing, my meagre possessions in my hands, and waited to go through the barred gate onto the wing. Another prisoner was standing at the gate, looking over at me.

'You're in for that murder, aren't you?' he said.

I looked at him, wondering where this was leading. 'Yeah,' I said.

'That was my mate,' he replied.

So this was where it was going: he was trying to put me in a corner.

'So fucking what?' I shot back, determined to nip this in the bud as quickly as possible. Sure enough, this kid backed down straight away. He must have thought he had some moral authority over the situation, but not as far as I was concerned. And I wasn't about to kick off my time on B Wing by backing down at the first sign of provocation.

And so we began to settle into the monotonous routine of prison life, where the day is mostly shaped around breakfast, lunch and tea. At eight o'clock each morning, prisoners are released for breakfast for thirty minutes then locked up again while movements, as they are called, permit selected prisoners to make their way to activities like work or education. At noon, prisoners return to the wing, when another brief period of unlock allows each landing to be called down for lunch before being locked up again. Throughout these periods, the prison carries out what are known as role counts to make sure no one has escaped or is missing. In the afternoon, at around one o'clock, activities resume; the sound of metal doors clanging and a growing chorus of voices indicates the time.

At around five o'clock, the same routine occurs. While prisoners return from activities, each landing is again called out to collect their tea (dinner). Only this time, there's evening association, around two hours when prisoners are allowed to mix, play pool, attend the gym or shower. This is also an opportunity to make phone calls, albeit expensive ones, if you don't mind waiting in a long queue. With around 200 prisoners located on B Wing, just getting five minutes can be a challenge. As for the prison food, it's shocking. The only bonus is that there is a canteen sheet from which prisoners can purchase additional items, though the range in HMP Hull consisted mostly of an unhealthy selection of overpriced sweets, crisps, chocolates and the odd tin of tuna.

I bumped into the kid who'd confronted me at the B Wing gates around the place and his tone had changed. He was polite now, telling me he never really liked Craig anyway and distancing himself from it. This was my first taste of confrontation inside and it confirmed what I already knew: I had no desire whatsoever to go looking for trouble, especially with my trial still to come, but if I backed down or showed fear, I'd leave myself vulnerable. So, things like that needed nipping in the bud.

I was fortunate in that I managed to get a single cell, an essential requirement given the amount of work I needed to do for our defence. Although they'd been bailed after being interviewed, Rory, John, Frankie and Ted had been charged with conspiracy to murder. The police were alleging that the attack was the result of a plan. I'd admitted that I waited outside the pub but the allegation that we had been plotting throughout the day had altered the implications for more than just me and Danny.

Having been left to pick up the pieces outside the prison, our families were also coming to terms with our situation. Hull prison wasn't far from where we lived, so our families and friends were able to take advantage of daily visits reserved for remand prisoners. Although it was still early days, the fact that I'd conceded to manslaughter meant I was going nowhere soon. Everyone knew it. But I tried to keep everybody upbeat by making sure I was jovial with my visitors whenever I could. The burden was ours, not our families'.

Danny was also receiving visits but it wasn't long before I noticed that his head would be permanently hung low or resting on his mother's lap. His family would give me the odd mucky look from their table.

'What's all that about?' I asked a friend who was visiting.

'There's a rumour going around that Danny's innocent,' they responded.

'So?' I replied, shrugging my shoulders.

Somehow, this rumour gained traction among our community and a group of misinformed sympathisers had jumped on the bandwagon.

'They're looking for witnesses to get him out,' said another visitor. 'They're putting pressure on everyone.'

Danny had not said anything to me, so I assumed his family were just overreacting to his low mood. But that thought was soon put to bed when I heard from a fellow prisoner that Danny had told him, 'I'm in here cos of that cunt.'

It was clear that Danny wasn't coping very well, but after hearing this, I felt I had to say something. Division was the last thing we needed. A few days passed and he eventually came into my cell, looking stressed.

'You all right?' I asked.

'No, I'm not all right!' he snapped, closing the door behind him. 'You killed him and you're just trying to drag me down!'

'Drag you down? I responded, confused. 'You know what I said.'

'All I did was kick Craig in the balls. Once!' he continued.

I shook my head. But I never tried to debate. Danny had somehow convinced himself that he was innocent. Though I shouldn't have been too surprised when he shouted and expected his own way. This had been the norm since we were kids. Offering him a way out was never considered an act of good will – it was always expected. I should have known better.

A short while later, I was leaning against the balcony outside my cell on the top floor, looking out. From the top landing you can see everything. Addicts scurrying from cell to cell, egos returning from the gym, stories of audacity, innocence and loss. The unwanted souls of society condensed inside a giant echo chamber that seems to cultivate more problems than it solves.

How the hell does someone put up with this for years on end? I thought to myself.

Wherever I was heading, I had a feeling it might not be with Danny by my side.

I landed a job working on the servery, where I would give other prisoners their food. It was a pretty routine job, until one day a guy on the wing came up to me and asked for more. I couldn't do it because there was hardly anything left and a long queue of hungry prisoners were lined up behind him. He wasn't happy about it.

'You fucking prick,' he said. 'Who do you think you are?'

I could feel my anger starting to rise, but managed to control myself and stay quiet. 'OK, yeah, no problem. No problem.'

The next morning, I woke up and thought, *I need to put this to bed.*

I'd spent time in young offenders' institutions, which aren't that different from prison in many ways. They can be very violent places – especially because they contain young people who aren't necessarily able to bring the same amount of self-control to violent situations as an adult would. Kids don't have the same kind of barriers when it comes to violence. I was no different – I'd been involved in a few fights during my time in a young offenders' institution. That's how things were settled and I didn't see this as being any different.

If I didn't square up to this guy, show him I wouldn't be pushed around, then anyone could have a go at me. So I went downstairs quite early and waited for him to come out. My plan, such as it was, was simply to confront him and say, 'Let's go to the showers and settle this.'

I was primed and ready, but after waiting for a considerable time I realised he wasn't coming out. He never showed his face in the end, so I walked away.

When I saw him later on, he came up to me and shook my hand. 'I didn't realise you were in for that murder,' he said, and we left it at that.

When I think back to that moment now, I consider myself extremely lucky that he didn't turn up that morning. Not because I was scared of getting hurt – I backed myself then, though anything can happen in a fight. But it was more the fact that, with my trial still to come and a lengthy stretch ahead of me, it could have sent me down a road quite different to the one I eventually walked down.

I'd been acting out of concern about how I would be perceived in the prison – how my peers would look on me. And these were legitimate concerns: once people know you're fair game, you've had it. But I would come to learn that offering to fight someone wasn't the only way to show strength and progress within the system.

★

I replaced Steph with Richard, a solicitor from Manchester with experience of complex cases. Richard would visit me several times a week and it was while corresponding with him that I realised there was a major weakness in my armoury. My writing was appalling. I could string a sentence together but never used capital letters or full stops. Nor could I distinguish between *there*, *their* and *they're*. If I wanted to communicate with lawyers and build a defence, I needed to improve. From that moment on, writing became an obsession, to the point that I had a permanent groove in my finger.

I also began to hit the gym in a major way. Prison life is pretty monotonous and the gym is a popular way to kill the time. But I made other, not always as popular changes too. I've always been the sort of person who is all or nothing, and I decided it was time for nothing in some aspects of my life. I stopped smoking and I resisted friendly offers of hooch (made from fermented fruit). I was done with alcohol.

Although I quit these vices overnight, despite having been a smoker since I was about fifteen, I had no withdrawal symptoms. I realised it wasn't the substances I'd been addicted to – it was the lifestyle. It had consumed me and was undoubtedly why I found it hard adjusting to a single cell on Saturday nights. I missed the buzz of that first drink, the feeling that we had no clue where the night would take us. I very soon found that I couldn't even listen to dance music any more as it reminded me too much of those Saturday nights out. It was unavoidable in the gym, where the pounding music soundtracked the workouts of convicted criminals and those awaiting trial in Hull, but where there was a choice, I didn't willingly listen to it again. Dance music, as innocuous as it might sound, was simply another vice that had to be quit.

I was fortunate to have some pleasures left, though. My cell had a view that overlooked the rooftops of my home city, a horizon on which the sun rested every evening. It was a small blessing in my fucked-up world.

CHAPTER 6

Divided We Fall

Danny threw the statement towards me and refused to take it back. We'd been sifting through a bundle of fresh evidence while sitting in the holding cells of Hull Crown Court. An anonymous witness had identified Danny jumping up and down on Craig's head multiple times and then punching someone in the crowd of onlookers as they tried to intervene.

'I know who it is,' said Danny as he paced up and down the cell. 'It's that cunt. I fucking know it.'

I tried to console him as his mind played out the statement's ramifications. But he was having none of it.

'What if I get life?' he kept repeating while shaking his head. 'What if I get life?'

Back at the prison, Jayne's visits had increased to around three a week. The situation had drawn us closer together, but seeing her pain close up and yet being powerless to help was tough to take. I felt terrible. On her own and still recovering from the aggravated burglary, Jayne just wanted me out. I wanted to be with her too. But I knew deep down it would be a long time before I saw freedom again. And matters were being made worse for Jayne outside the prison walls, where I could do nothing to help.

'Some of his relatives had a go at me last night,' said Jayne. 'They're saying it's your fault he's locked up.'

Although they'd heard eye-witness accounts that confirmed Danny's culpability, they'd refused to accept it and had maintained the idea that his predicament was my fault.

I began spending time in the prison library, sifting through law books and reading Archbold, a criminal law reference book for legal professionals. I wanted to learn about the various defences to murder and wondered whether provocation could form part of my defence. There was no elaborate plan and no intention to kill, and, as I scrolled through the pages of each book, I was confident that these facts would count for something. Then I came across a phrase from a judgement that caught my eye: 'In English law, a defendant may be convicted of murder who is in no ordinary sense a murderer.'

On further scrutiny, I learned that there are two ways that a British citizen can be convicted of murder: either by intending to kill or by intending to cause serious bodily harm. Suddenly, the prospect of a murder conviction appeared more ominously on the horizon.

In the meantime, Rory and my other three co-defendants had had their charges dropped for conspiracy to murder. Their elimination from the inquiries came just two days after Ted had strolled into a police station to provide another statement.

'It doesn't look good,' I said to Danny as we headed back to the wing from our visits.

'Wonder what it says?' he replied, without a trace of anxiety.

'Well, it's not about a missing dog, is it?'

Unflustered, Danny strolled off to join his cellmate for a game of cards.

Sure enough, when I finally got to see it, Ted's statement confirmed what I'd suspected it would. Its content destroyed my chances of achieving a manslaughter conviction.

It was pointless saying anything to Danny. The message had been delivered.

After spending the morning in the library, I returned to the wing as usual with a couple of books tucked under my arm. As I walked through B Wing gates, I was approached by a couple of excited prisoners bearing news that Danny had left the prison.

'He's a grass, mate!' said one.

'No one gets bail for murder!' said the other.

I brushed aside their words of warning while an associate calmly informed me that Danny's relatives had put up £70,000 to secure his bail. It was 20 June, we were seven weeks into remand, and Danny, the friend who had stood with me for the best part of twenty years, was gone.

When you're facing the prospect of serving an extremely long time in prison, nothing much else enters your mind apart from how to reduce its impact. Even the 7/7 bombings in London, a terrorist attack that killed 52 people and injured hundreds more, barely caught my attention as the wreckage flashed across TV screens throughout the summer months of 2005.

Frequent visits from Jayne, often the first to arrive in a long line of eager visitors, at least offered me something to look forward to. Watching her stroll into the visits hall with her beautiful smile never failed to remind me of how lucky I was to have her. Putting aside the circumstances under which we were now courting, and with nothing between us but a knee-high coffee table, we started to get to know each other again. Irritatingly for the visits staff, she was often the last to leave too, as we would drag out the final few moments of each visit by embracing and avoiding eye contact with the officers. Still, if watching Jayne arrive was uplifting, watching her leave was a constant reminder of the fool I'd been.

On 12 July, the autopsy report arrived. The pathologist had concluded that the cause of death was head injuries. That seemed inevitable, but the implications of that finding would later turn out to have profound consequences. What was more immediately compelling was the catalogue of injuries. As I read the report, and absorbed the extent of the injuries and the violence of the attack, I began to feel unsettled. I thought about what a jury would make of us – what I would make of me, if I were in their place.

Contemplating an image of me at the scene, one that the jury would also form, gave me a different perspective on my violence. I didn't like what I saw. But there was no getting away from it: it was me. What I had done suddenly seemed so visceral and real to me. Was this who I really was? Was this who I really wanted to be?

Meanwhile, Jacob Clifton, one of the alleged perpetrators of the aggravated burglary on Jayne's flat, had been remanded to HMP Hull and found himself on the wing next to mine. I received a message, scribbled on a piece of paper. Jacob denied entering my home to attack the occupants but conceded he'd waited outside while Craig entered. He was undoubtedly protecting himself from a lengthy prison sentence. But he did offer to attend court to provide evidence about Craig's involvement and confirmed that Craig had been looking for me while armed with a hammer.

I was advised by my lawyer that, since Danny had been granted bail, if I could stump up the money I would have a reasonable chance for bail too. A family member even offered to provide me with the funds. It was tempting, the prospect of tasting freedom, but I declined the offer. Although Danny was free, he'd been placed in a bail hostel 60 miles away and barred from entering Hull. And since I was facing a prison sentence for at least a manslaughter conviction, the thought of isolating myself in another city miles from my family would only exacerbate my problems and make it harder for Jayne.

By now, my hopes for the legal defence of provocation had faded. Because I'd waited outside the pub and engaged in a coordinated, albeit unsophisticated approach, it meant the assault was premeditated, a term that altered my perception once its legal meaning had been explained to me. Having said that, I certainly felt provoked in the normal sense of the word. It's not every day that your partner is randomly attacked in your home by a person who is then said to be looking for you because the police had failed to arrest him. This is not to justify what happened. My only remaining hope at that point was that Jacob's evidence might be used as mitigation on sentencing. According to Richard, if I was convicted of murder I would be facing up to 22 years.

At a pretrial hearing, which is used to determine the admissibility of evidence and decide on other legal issues, the trial date had been set for 24 Oct 2005 and was to be presided over by The Honourable Mr Justice Crane, a High

Court judge. Danny was sitting next to me at the hearing, listening intently. While our lawyers communicated in a different language, I glanced his way. Although he never acknowledged me, I felt sorry him. With his facial expression matching the slope of his shoulders, I could tell he was desperately hoping, like me, that a miracle would happen and he would suddenly walk free.

Back at the prison, someone loaned me *The Wall*, the 1970s Pink Floyd album about a rock singer becoming isolated and struggling to come to terms with his father's death. Some of the tracks are deep, so it probably wasn't an ideal choice given my situation. But the lyrics in one of the songs, 'Together we stand, divided we fall', caught my attention as I lay on my bed, contemplating how to navigate the least painful route to hell. Even if Danny and I were convicted, our fall would be far worse if we couldn't find a way to work together.

Rory was a lifelong friend of ours so he made a good candidate for mediation. I persuaded him to visit Danny in Leeds, where he was staying at his bail hostel. But despite the fact that Rory was actually present at the scene of our crime, Danny held his stance and continued to blame me.

'But you ran him over!' Rory protested.

Danny shook his head. 'You don't understand.'

In the end, Rory returned to Hull confused and with nothing to show for his efforts.

Danny and I were not career criminals. We worked hard and paid our taxes, so neither of us was conditioned to prison life, let alone to serving long sentences. But we did have a criminal edge to our lifestyles. Since we were kids, we had used violence to settle disputes and relied on the rules of the street to evade justice. This time, although we never intended the outcome, our actions had come back to bite us in a devastating way. I was scared too and didn't want to spend one more day in prison, but the circumstances we found ourselves in were entirely of our own making.

Given it was my grudge, I was still prepared to make the biggest compromise, but when Jayne walked into the visits hall one day with her face bruised and scratched, a line had been crossed. She'd been attacked by some of his associates while out on her own.

I'd chosen to take the hit out of loyalty, not because I felt I was any more guilty than Danny. Yet my loyalty, which was once his greatest asset, had become my greatest burden. Danny had not only gone back on his word almost immediately after we'd shaken hands; he'd positioned himself as my adversary. It was the last the thing we needed but I had to acknowledge it. I sent him a message: 'You get yourself out of it and I'll get myself out of it.'

A week before the trial, we had another court appearance. Mr Justice Crane ruled that the anonymous witnesses could not give evidence in court unless they revealed their identity. Danny lifted his head with a sense of hope. It meant the anonymous witness who had identified Danny jumping up and down on Craig's head multiple times might be reluctant to reveal their identity and so be unable to give evidence.

He needed something. A forensic analysis of his clothing, which had been found hidden behind his garden shed, had been described as 'conclusive' by the prosecuting counsel. He'd also breached his bail conditions after failing a breathalyser test. Confused at how Danny had managed to secure bail in the first place, Mr Justice Crane refused a second application and sent him back to HMP Hull.

Danny and I remained cordial with one another as we waited in the holding cells before returning to our separate wings. If damage limitation was the priority, then working together on certain aspects of our case was far more important than finding points of disagreement. Still, I could no longer trust him. Although the Crown Prosecution Service had decided not to call Ted as a witness to court, his statement could still be used against me if he were to be summoned through Danny's defence team. With this in mind, I let Danny know that a friend of mine had recorded Ted admitting that he'd been pressured to make the statement.

Danny never responded. I just heard him sigh as he realised that he could no longer risk using Ted's statement.

This was the position I now found myself in: rather than assisting Danny, I was using tactics to limit his potential to cause me damage.

CHAPTER 7

A Window into Our Souls

Representing the Crown, Mr Campbell QC delivered his opening speech to the jury while they shook their heads in disgust. He was good. Bringing his speech to a climax, he turned and pointed towards the two of us shifting uncomfortably in the dock. 'Steven Gallant and Daniel McCallister, they are responsible . . .' he declared while looking directly at us.

I'll never forget those eyes. It was like he was staring straight into our souls. I wanted to look away but I held my gaze as a well-timed crescendo, followed by a pause in his speech, directed the jury's attention towards us. I reassured myself: *It's all part of the act. We'll get our chance.*

But after a week of sitting through Mr Campbell's meticulous presentation, our situations were clarified. Danny was finished and I wasn't far behind him.

To lower the threshold of culpability, Mr Campbell was using a legal principle called joint enterprise. It meant that if the jury found there was a common purpose and we each engaged in that purpose with an intention to cause serious bodily harm, and Craig died as a result of that harm, then we would both be guilty of murder. It would not matter who struck which blows. The jury only had to find that we acted together with the same foresight and intention. So even if Danny was found, for example, only to have held someone back in the crowd while I carried out the deed, provided the jury were satisfied that all other requirements had been proven, he would still be guilty of murder.

As it turned out, the anonymous witness who'd described Danny attacking Craig had opted to reveal his identity and give evidence in court. During his testimony, he also alleged that he was the bystander Danny had punched during the violence. But it was irrelevant in the wider context. So when the forensics analysis of the blood found on Danny's clothing corresponded with the actions of kicking and stamping, it sealed his fate.

Even though the pathologist had informed the court that there was no evidence to say which blows had caused death, I could hardly argue that my actions had not in some way contributed. I'd already confessed as much, so I was prepared to serve time for manslaughter if that option arose. But as I never intended to kill, and thought that the jury would be left to determine my level of intent, putting my hands up to the moral equivalent of murdering someone seemed suicidal. I knew I was pushing it, but confronted with the prospect of never seeing daylight again, I was getting nervous. Mr Campbell was arguing that Danny and I had, at the least, intended to cause serious bodily harm, which equates to murder in British law. If Mr Campbell could prove this, we would be convicted as if we had intended to kill and be condemned to the only available option to the judge – a mandatory life sentence.

True to his word, Jacob Clifton did show up to give evidence on my behalf. But even truer to his habit, he did so under the influence of drugs. As a result, he was dismissed by my defence team.

Yet something far more unfavourable was about to occur. During the trial, the issue of manslaughter was discussed between counsel, but it was not progressed. Suddenly, my assertion that I'd only intended to cause some harm, the mental aspect for manslaughter, had become worthless. I was acutely aware that this meant either accepting a life sentence there and then or maintaining a lack of intent for a murder conviction. Faced with this stark choice, I stepped into the witness box.

It was brief. After I repeated what I'd already divulged in my original statement and explained that my violence was mine alone, Mr Campbell asked me who was responsible for Craig's death.

'I can't say, because I walked off and I didn't see anybody else make any physical contact with him,' I replied, trying not to directly implicate Danny while hoping the jury would somehow accept a lack of intent.

When asked about my comment 'someone fell over us', I denied it happened. I'd made it up, for sure, but it had become more than just a phrase to me. It had come to symbolise everything that was wrong with my priorities. And yet, when I denied it happened, I still cringed inside.

Danny was up next and performed as I'd expected.

'Just blood all over the place, just red, absolutely. If I close my eyes now, I can see it. There was blood all over his face.' He went on to say that while I was attacking Craig, he was trying but struggling to pull me off, calling for me to stop. And in the midst of this, someone pushed him and he did a tipple tail, perhaps standing on Craig in the process.

'There has to be a lot of blood in your defence, doesn't there?' probed Mr Campbell.

For almost two days, he tore Danny's defence to pieces, a task made significantly easier by the meddling of others while Danny had buried his head in the sand. The more pressure Danny came under, the more he tried to deflect attention towards me: 'He's a dangerous man . . . My girlfriend told me to stop knocking around with him.'

My barrister, Kate Blackwell, turned to face me. 'He's gone,' she mouthed under her breath.

While it wasn't the most enjoyable experience watching Danny apply the finishing touches to our fate, it was just as sad watching the embers of a twenty-year friendship fade to nothing. What had happened to our leader, the person I thought I knew so well? Mr Campbell wasn't cross-examining an adult; he was peering into the mind of the seven-year-old boy I'd met all those years ago on a beach, refusing to take responsibility.

I glanced over to the public gallery as the truth filled the courtroom, stiffening the air like a freezing mist. It was over – for both of us. After Mr Justice Crane had completed his summing up, the jury disappeared to determine our fate. They weren't long.

I'd given up trying to gauge their intentions. I just knew. I looked at Jayne. We smiled at each other, as we had done throughout. This was the last time. When the jury were asked for their verdict on 'Steven Gallant', the foreman cried, 'Guilty!'

Jayne screamed and ran out of the court. I remained calm, but only to reassure my family that I was OK.

A short while later Danny followed me to the gallows.

For taking Craig's life, the judge gave us each a life sentence with a minimum tariff of 17 years.

Throughout my time on remand and during the trial, I disagreed with various aspects of other people's behaviour and the case, but I never disagreed with Mr Justice Crane's closing statement: 'Saint or sinner, everyone has the right not to be killed in the way that man was on that night.'

CHAPTER 8

Milk and Biscuits

'Come on, Stevie,' urged Officer Mullins after he had cracked open my door. 'You might as well get back to work. Take your mind off things.'

He had a point. Lying on my bed, wallowing in self-pity, was no way to begin a life sentence. So back I went.

My promotion to a life-sentence prisoner meant I was to be transferred to HMP Frankland, a category A prison and one of the toughest in the country. I'd heard stories about Frankland but I was in no frame of mind to start thinking about how my future might pan out. I was defeated, my mental energy sapped. The only saving grace was that since my transfer was going to take a while, Jayne and I were able to take advantage of local visits, albeit now reduced to once a fortnight.

As the months rolled into 2006, I returned to the gym and slowly began to rebuild my strength. For the first time in years, I'd been sober for an extended period of time. The chemicals that had clouded my judgement had gone and I was able to focus with more clarity. The library also remained my place of worship as I continued digging into law books and anything educational. After undergoing an intense experience of powerlessness, aided by my lack of knowledge, I knew the only way I could regain some control over my life and ultimately achieve my freedom was to continue learning. There may have been no immediate escape from my surroundings but at least I could control something.

With fewer distractions, my attention shifted towards Jayne. I'd put my friends first on endless nights out over the years and yet Jayne had stuck by me and stood up to our antagonists mostly on her own. And where were my friends now? Yet another reminder of the fool I'd been.

Over the long, hot summer of 2006, Jayne breezed faithfully in and out of the visits hall bearing news from the free world and, for the first time in my life, it truly hit me. Everything I'd ever wanted in a woman had been right in front of me all along. I'd fallen in love with her again.

And just when I'd finally had my eyes opened, the inevitable arose. That knee-high coffee table between us in the visits hall had become more than just something on which to place our drinks. It was an impenetrable barrier to our intimacy. And now that I had been convicted, the state had tightened its noose and something snapped.

Jayne started to cry. 'I can't do this any more,' she sobbed while wiping her tears.

'What?' I replied.

'I can't do it, Steve.'

There was silence while my brain tried to process the implications. An image of someone being intimate with Jayne flashed through my mind. I knew it wasn't her immediate aim but it was certain that she would meet someone else. Just like she had for me, she would be loyal to him, stroke his head and flash him that beautiful smile.

In desperation, I said, 'But I did it for you!'

Jayne shook her head. 'I asked you not to do anything,' she responded sternly.

I racked my brain, hoping to come back with some-thing, anything, to make Jayne question her decision. But I had nothing.

After an awkward visit, I returned to B Wing, headed straight to my cell and locked the door behind me.

Later that evening, with Jayne's words ringing in my ears, I leaned against the bars of my cell window and watched the sun set over the rooftops of East Hull. Pigeons cooed overhead; the odd shout from a neighbour breached the stillness.

She did ask me not to do anything, I recalled solemnly. And I didn't just do it for her. I was worried about what my mates would think if I didn't react with aggression. And four weeks before she was attacked, I'd left Jayne on her own when I'd moved to my mother's. Now I expected her to wait around while I completed a sentence that had no natural end.

Just as I had taken my freedom for granted, so too had I failed to fully appreciate Jayne's love. While I grad-ually swallowed whatever dignity I had left, I accepted it wasn't just Hull I might never see again. After the sun had disappeared below the skyline, I wrote Jayne a letter that concluded: 'We should at least end on a good note.'

At the end of her final visit we embraced tightly, then, after one last tear, Jayne walked out of the prison, and out of my life.

Almost immediately after Jayne's departure, I found myself in the segregation unit. During Jayne's final visit, when she tenderly put her hand upon my arm, a female prison officer had shouted at us across the visits hall to stop. We reluctantly relented but I was furious. I parked it, so as not to interfere with saying goodbye to Jayne.

On the way out from the visits room, I saw this officer again and called her fat and jealous, to the amusement of other prisoners. In no other circumstance would it have bothered me but after watching Jayne walk out of my life for good and irritated by the insensitivity of this officer, it just came out of me. I was soon nicked and put in the seg unit. As far down as recent events had brought me, this was a new low.

Underneath C Wing, the cells are like dungeons, with arched ceilings and large porous bricks. It was dark in there – the only window was opaque, high up in the arched roof with bars across it. I couldn't see out of it and barely any light came in from it. And then there was the cold and damp, with ants, woodlice and silverfish crawling about the place.

So this is what prison is, I thought to myself, all alone in the world. Or so I thought.

'Stevie G!' called a muffled voice from the cell next door.

I raised my head. 'Who's that?'

'Is that you?'

'Who is it?'

'Come t'door,' he demanded. 'It's Robby.'

At the base of the door was a half-inch gap so I sprawled out on the hard surface, bringing myself significantly closer to the familiar fusty odour that marks every cell. Then again, any floor that's lain there for as long as this one had is not going to smell too pretty. Still, having someone to talk to is vastly more important than any aroma when you're feeling down. Especially when you know them.

Robby was a friend from my council estate but, like so many of the kids I'd been brought up with from that era, he'd become heavily addicted to heroin. He'd only been released that morning, so I was double-surprised to hear his voice. After telling me how he'd managed to breach his bail, Robby and I made the most of our situation and chatted for several hours. I felt envious of his comparatively imminent return to freedom.

'You don't realise what you've got,' I'd said to him.

He just laughed. A cold, mirthless, knowing laugh.

After my arm had turned numb and I'd blown away every ant that dared encroach into my personal space, I picked myself up and climbed onto the bed to retreat under my covers. I knew I was on my way to a dark place and would need all the strength I could muster.

Slumped like a boxer in their corner of the ring, my aggression had fizzled to nothing. Violence had followed me round my whole life but where had it got me? Violence had cost me my freedom and the most important thing in my life. The verbal abuse I'd just unleashed on the prison officer had compounded my misery, left me festering in nothing better than a dungeon in the pit of the prison.

Something had to change. If I was going to have any sort of future within this system, and perhaps even one day outside it, I was going to need to be able to control my capacity for violence in all its forms. To be able to turn the other cheek, even under provocation. I had no idea then what challenges lay ahead at HMP Frankland and beyond, nor what sort of men would test the promise I was about to make to myself. But I knew I had to make this change. So I went ahead and swore to myself most solemnly.

I vowed never to use violence again.

The next day, I woke with a raging headache, like my brain was pushing against the back of my eyeballs. I could just about tolerate the nightlight as I moped around the cell with a blanket over my shoulders. As I revisited every facet of my life during those miserable hours, I accepted that it wasn't other people that beat me, it was me. The real delusion was the ideas I'd been living under, blindly following them like a sacred text. Over thirty witnesses at the scene and the only person who gave evidence against me was the one I most trusted. How did I make such a mistake? I needed to know.

But how do you scale a mountain that's covered in dense mist, strewn with deep crevices and teeming with dangerous animals? That glimpse into a treacherous world gave me an insight into why so many prisoners take drugs. It means they can escape reality. Maybe that's why Robby laughed? He could lose himself in bliss while everyone else suffered. But that wasn't an option for me. Like violence, drugs had been part of the problem. If I wanted to make it, I needed a clear mind, if only to see where each foot was about to tread.

Later that day, I heard the bolt unfasten and the door was pushed open, the light from the corridor making me squint as it drew in behind a silhouette.

'You in for killing that guy?' asked the prison officer standing there.

I nodded. My headache intensified.

'Here,' he beckoned while holding out his arms. 'Here's some milk and some biscuits.'

I took the milk and asked him to share half the biscuits with Robby.

Given my situation, I appreciated this small act of compassion. But I also felt uneasy. This wasn't the first time I'd experienced this kind of gesture, a pat on the back like I'd volunteered, as if I'd made a conscious decision to throw away my life.

Now that I had some proper milk, I made a cup of tea. Prison teabags taste foul, but it soothed my headache and eventually allowed me to consider the one remaining priority I had left – my family. Peacefully and with dignity, they had remained firmly by my side as I tried to navigate the grim after-effects of my actions. My sisters, brother, Mum, Dad, even my grandmother – they had visited regularly during my time in HMP Hull, and they were the ones who were going to be there till the end, travelling up and down the country and making sacrifices on my behalf. At least I had them.

PART III

Category A:
HMP Frankland

CHAPTER 9

Welcome to Frankland

Located in County Durham in the north east, HMP Frankland is one of the eight high-security prisons in England that are home to category A prisoners, those who pose the greatest threat to the public or national security if they were to escape. As such, Frankland houses some of the most dangerous men in the country. Serial killers, contract killers, drug smugglers, terrorists and the criminally insane – you name it, it's there. When I arrived in late 2006, the main population consisted of around 200 prisoners, housed on two open-plan, L-shaped wings, G and F, located opposite each other. Sex offenders and child killers were housed in separate buildings, isolated from the main population for their own protection.

At the rear of G Wing lay another self-contained building called Westgate, a specialist unit that treated men diagnosed as psychopaths, sociopaths or as having dangerous or severe personality disorders. For those who do manage to complete their treatment, they are typically released back into the main prison population to continue serving their sentence. No doubt to see how they cope.

With plenty to think about as I headed down to my new home in G Wing with my belongings, I began to wonder whether the decision to send me here had been some kind of mistake. By the time I reached the entrance to G Wing, at least one thing was clear. Once inside Frankland, there is no escape. The layers of steel, concrete, fencing, razor wire and the sense of depth you experience as you eventually reach your living quarters leave you in no doubt of that. Even if you had access to a helicopter, it would be impossible to land since the exercise yards are crisscrossed with steel wire. And dangling a rope between the wires would not work either, since your escape vehicle would trigger a rapid response from the authorities. So long as you're not serving a whole-life term, the only way you can reach freedom again is through the front gate.

Oh, and it's dull. With not even a blade of grass on which to rest your gaze, the lack of colour in the vicinity of G and F wings merely adds to the impression that the place was built for hatred, hardened criminals and psychopaths. So I walked onto G Wing expecting the worst.

As the new person arriving in the prison, you have a very real sense that all eyes are on you. Everyone's looking, checking out the new arrival – probing for any signs of weakness. Or at least that's what it feels like. As I arrived on my landing, there were a lot of guys looking over, particularly some lads who I would later discover were part of a black gang that was a major force on the wing. I could feel their gaze on me; one lad in particular was eyeballing me. It wasn't all that long ago that I would have had a good look back, let him know I wasn't fazed at all by him. But with my recently made promise to renounce violence fresh in my mind, I decided to try to put into practice the idea of turning the other cheek.

Was I scared? At that stage of my life I felt very confident of being able to carry myself physically but I was definitely wary. You've got to be on your guard in prison and it doesn't matter what kind of shape you're in if a gang sets about you or someone attacks you from behind.

At one point, with the stares continuing, I did allow myself one good look at my eyeballer, just to let him know I wasn't someone he could easily push over. That's the irony of prison environments; doing nothing could also leave you a target. I could see him whispering with his friends, his eyes on me, talking about me. It brought to mind the video I'd watched about Frankland just before I left Hull, in which the narrator said, 'With such a colourful mix of personalities, there are inevitable squabbles.'

Is this how they start? I thought to myself. I knew I would have to be ready.

Then, a few days later, one of his friends, who was also my neighbour, offered me some food he'd cooked. I politely declined. But after that, the tense atmosphere between me and the eyeballer dissipated.

Yet, despite this odd interaction during the first week or so, as I went about completing my induction, which included visits to the gym, healthcare and other departments a prisoner might need to familiarise themselves with, I was struck by the calm atmosphere at Frankland. Another prisoner told me the place had been quiet for a few months, except for the odd skirmish.

'Watch out for him, though, mate,' this prisoner warned me under his breath while we waited in the dinner queue. 'He's been in about twenty years. Right fucking nutcase.'

'Who's that?' I asked.

'Zane Patton,' he replied. 'The one with the curtains.'

I walked off, wondering who this person was, and told myself to keep an eye out for the lump with the curtains.

With around twenty officers strategically positioned across the wing, the prospect of a sustained fight seemed unlikely. Until I saw a group of the black gang attack a Scottish lad within my first few weeks. It was over an unpaid drug debt, one of the biggest causes of violence and bullying in the system, and resulted in the Scotsman having his cell burnt out. This involved putting newspaper inside a cardboard box, setting it alight and placing it under his bed.

Having no desire to take drugs and sensing that I might not have to physically battle my way through Frankland after all, I felt relieved. Still, even though I was done with violence, I knew I was bound to be tested and I had to be prepared to defend myself. I was not overly afraid of being hurt; it was the thought of landing another charge that scared me. Category A prisoners are generally desensitised to higher levels of violence, so a simple disagreement can turn into a fight for your life, or a murder charge, which, for me, would mean remaining in prison for the rest of my life.

Pool and snooker aside, the lack of wing activities was noticeable. Unlike at Hull, however, there were four kitchens on the wing with two cookers in each and large freezers dotted about the place, a legacy from when category A prisons held high numbers of IRA prisoners. Apparently, Irish officials wanted to make sure they were looked after. Cooking, I soon realised, was a primary pastime at Frankland.

Boredom, then, was one of the biggest challenges that faced an inmate at Frankland. And in such an environment, idle time offered all sorts of scope for building unhealthy relationships and habits. I decided to keep myself busy and focus on education. I didn't have a qualification to my name, so I enrolled in maths, English, information and communications technology courses and, as time went on, anything else that caught my fancy.

Most of my time was now spent in the education block. I'd imagined it would be a popular way to kill time inside but surprisingly there were only three or four students in each class. Though at least this gave me more opportunities to pick the teachers' brains. Just being curious, I once asked the English teacher whether she thought it was possible that I might be able to write a book one day.

'No,' she replied, lifting her head to glance at me.

She wasn't being rude. In fact, this teacher had dedicated her life to educating prisoners. She was just being realistic. The class was for students on Entry Level 1, the most basic level for English.

During my enrolment, I also noticed a subject called philosophy. Out of curiosity, I signed up. With plenty of time on my hands and my mind ripe for learning and at the peak of introspection, philosophy turned out to be perfect. And not just for me.

'I don't believe in God,' I blurted out during a discussion on religion.

'That don't mean there isn't one,' interrupted Jez Deaffern, a larger-than-life Welsh–Mancunian who was sitting next to me on the first day of induction.

Did I say there isn't one? I thought to myself.

Jez had arrived at Frankland a couple of days after me but seemed to know everyone. He was a high-risk, category A prisoner, serving 25 years for drug smuggling. Yet his persona and form misrepresented him. Jez was a deep thinker and had a thirst for knowledge.

'It's about the journey, not just the destination,' he remarked during one of our early conversations.

We ended up taking many of our discussions back to the wing and struck up a friendship.

It didn't take me long to discover who Zane Patton was.

I was walking along the landing one day when I bumped into someone by accident. 'Sorry, mate,' I responded reflexively.

'Fucking prick,' he growled under his breath as he continued walking without even turning to look at me.

When I was warned about him, I'd got the impression he was going to be some big guy with a bent nose, so I was surprised to find that Zane, with his relatively small stature and his blond curtains drooping below his ears, looked more like someone out of a nineties boy band. But, of course, you should never judge a book by its cover.

Every now and then, I would see the biggest and most powerful guys on the wing, themselves notorious individuals, sporting a black eye for upsetting Zane's view of the world. As I observed these incidents and heard the stories about Zane's super-human confidence, I wondered about his life and the events that had brought him there. His reputation was not gained for nothing. Reviled by many, revered by the impressionable and feared by all, Zane was a shark, fearlessly circling the system while picking off his prey. Unsurprisingly, during his encounters across the cat A system, spanning nearly two decades, he had managed to establish some deadly enemies, other sharks who were also circling the system. Usually, Zane would just sit at the back of the wing with his back to the wall, reading his daily newspaper. With the odd cursory glance, he was undoubtedly keeping an eye open for these other sharks.

Zane had called me a 'fucking prick', which might have meant nothing in the grand scheme of things or it might mean he'd taken a bit of a dislike to me. You can never tell with the most dangerous prisoners, so it was something to be aware of, just to be on my guard.

I saw one of my first examples of a 'squabble' in action when I witnessed one prisoner, part of the black gang, attack another, a white prisoner, who smashed a tomato sauce bottle to use as a weapon in self-defence to fight him off. This latter guy was moved off onto another wing and things seemed to calm down after that.

A couple of days later, I was in the gym. I nipped off for a bathroom break, and on my way to the toilets I noticed the instigator of the attack in front of me, walking in and looking back at me. I'd never spoken to him before and this seemed a bit odd. My instincts sensed trouble but I knew I had to stay calm.

As I walked over to the toilet he went straight for the sink and just stood next to it, his hand in his pocket. He was very clearly letting me know he had a knife in his pocket. *Don't try it,* he seemed to be saying. Not that I was about to. I very calmly walked over to the sink and washed my hands. He never moved his hand from his pocket, just kept his eyes on me. He was a big, thick-set guy and clearly paranoid too; I knew that one wrong move would spell trouble. I was acutely aware of his presence and posture, but I couldn't let him see that. Instead, I calmly dried off and walked out, letting him know there was no threat from me.

He must have thought I knew the guy he'd attacked, or perhaps that I'd been paid to carry out a hit on him. But I would soon learn that these little instances happened all the time in prison. Usually they come to nothing. Often they're just little things, which might have nothing at all to do with you, but you've just got to have your wits about you.

In early 2007, I received news from my family back home that Robby, my neighbour from the seg unit back in HMP Hull, had hanged himself. It took me by surprise. He was a free man at the time. I just didn't get it. I found myself running over our conversation, when I'd thought he didn't appreciate his freedom. Maybe that was why he'd laughed at me. My naivety. Robby may have been physically free but mentally he was still trapped in his own prison.

The idea that we can be imprisoned by our own minds was beginning to gain considerable traction with me. I'd started to notice how some of those around me had been negatively impacted by the ideas that underpin prison culture. While standing in the dinner queue one day, a lifer who'd been at Frankland for eighteen years told me he'd steadfastly refused to enter a room with a psychologist or a probation officer, which was crucial to his eventual freedom, because he was worried that other prisoners would think he was a grass. As a result of this self-defeating notion, he was still stuck in a category A prison many years beyond his tariff expiry date.

But if being inside came with the risk of becoming further imprisoned by my mind, it also offered the chance to broaden it. By now, I'd spent months immersed in the wisdom of philosophers throughout history in the education block. It made me realise how much my lack of education and exposure to influences outside my social circle had been holding me back.

I'd become interested in the seeds of Western Enlightenment thinking, a turning point in Europe's history when rationality and reason began to challenge ignorance, superstition and religious dogma. When I looked back at the cruelty and violence perpetrated in the name of belief, what was most interesting to me was that these people didn't carry out these acts because they were evil; on the whole, they did it because they thought they were doing society a favour. They were so blinded by the dominant ideology of their time that burning people at the stake was seen as an act of mercy.

Philosophers like René Descartes and scientists like Galileo questioned the prevailing ideas of their time. They eventually pulled humanity in a different direction, altered the trajectory of history and helped lay the foundations of today's freedoms and scientific advances. And they carried out their work in the face of being severely punished (as Galileo was) or burnt at the stake (as many others were). Had they not taken these risks and stirred the imaginations of following generations, ideas like tolerance, reason and humanity might never have taken hold and we might well have remained in the dark ages, 'mercifully' drowning innocent women or setting fire to the poor for daring to think outside the box.

But how susceptible did the human mind remain to adverse ideas? And how safe were the masses from collective madness for a 'good' cause?

These were the sort of ideas I was discussing with Jez on the way back to G Wing from the education block when he was called over by Tion, another inmate. I said my 'see you later' to Jez and walked off.

Tion was a convert known for having extreme religious views and acting on them. The previous day, he and Jez had had a disagreement over something trivial. So trivial, in fact, that they had shaken hands on it and put it to bed. Or at least, that's what Jez thought as he averted his gaze and turned to walk away. Without warning, Tion lunged at him and stabbed him in the neck.

A scuffle broke out, followed by a spike of energy as officers scrambled to break them up. When a fight breaks out on a prison wing, there's a very distinctive sound – officers running, the jangle of keys. This one was over as quick as it began and Tion was dragged kicking and screaming to the segregation unit. The stab wound was less than an inch from Jez's jugular vein.

I soon realised that the appearance of calmness was exactly that. Underneath the surface, Frankland's wings were volatile places. The incident with Jez is how a lot of violence plays out in category A prisons. With so many unpredictable prisoners confined under one roof, the chance of coming across someone equally dangerous is high. Assuming then that danger is always present, you give away less: no fears, no weaknesses, no intentions, nothing. The less your perceived or real enemy knows about you, the better your chance of survival. It's the same with other rule-breaking activities, like the sale of drugs, which occur but go very much unnoticed to the untrained eye. With these tensions and interactions between prisoners happening daily and during a limited window of time, they become highly refined to the point of looking ordinary.

Following a standoff that left the officers nervously watching from the sidelines, the incident with Tion almost led to a conflict between a large group of black lads and Jez's mates. But with Tion taken to the segregation unit, it remained just one of a few relatively minor incidents that would begin to build tension.

For my part, I hadn't been present when things had kicked off. If I'd been in the middle of it, it would have been very difficult not to get involved and help Jez out. It made me think that choosing to avoid violence was one thing, but prison life was going to mean there would be times when there might be no choice but to use violence in self-defence. Luck, I would soon discover – managing not to be in the wrong place at the wrong time – would also play its part.

Zane, however, was fuming. 'Listen, you,' he growled at Jez. 'Next time you have trouble with any of them lot, you come and get me. All right?'

CHAPTER 10

Rising Tensions

The social dynamics of a prison environment can be delicate at the best of times. It only takes the arrival of one or two high-profile prisoners to tip the balance into disruptiveness, such is the prevalence of peer influence in prisons. And when a big shift happens it can have profound consequences. I would come to learn that these arrivals were rare. And rarer still were the occasions when two such shifts would come along at once.

Frankland had been reasonably quiet since Christmas 2006, but throughout the spring of 2007 a large number of high-profile white British prisoners landed on G Wing and began to establish themselves. Their arrival coincided with the departure of several black prisoners who had previously held some sway. In just a matter of months, the fluctuating tides of the prison system had noticeably shifted the balance of power into the hands of the white majority.

But remarkably, this change to the make-up of Frankland's prison population, while large by any standard, was about to be dwarfed by a far more significant event, one that would send shockwaves across the prison system and drastically alter its fabric forever. That was the arrival of the first true wave of Islamist terrorists and their sympathisers into Frankland and the other category A prisons. Fuelled by Western interventions in Afghanistan and Iraq, the tentacles of radical Islamist ideology had long since reached UK shores and its impact was now being felt. The result was a succession of terrorist attacks, foiled plots and a growing number of successful convictions for terrorism-related offences. To politicians and the public, the 7/7 bombings in London in July 2005 and another failed terrorist plot later that same month were a wake-up call for the UK. To the propagators and adherents of extremist ideologies, it merely vindicated their efforts, emboldened their cause and helped to fill their hidden ranks.

While the London bombings in 2005 hardly caught my attention when I was on remand awaiting trial, they had not been missed by the prison population at large, including the recent arrivals to G Wing. Frankland had always held terrorists from one cause or another, and at the time of my arrival, there were a handful of prisoners convicted of terrorism offences pre-2005. But such was the media prominence of the 7/7 attack that the profile of any terrorist who landed at Frankland following convictions from that date was significantly elevated.

The first Islamic extremist to arrive was Hussain Osman. He'd been convicted of the botched terrorist attack at Shepherd's Bush tube station on 21 July 2005 and sentenced to 40 years.

Taking offence at his presence on the wing, certain prisoners wanted rid of him: 'Fucking trying to kill our people, eh?'

'At least we used to give a warning,' protested Tommy, an ex-IRA member who had carried out contract killings.

Two young men, Johnno and Birchy, had volunteered to make an example of Osman using chivs (makeshift knives). I knew Birchy from HMP Hull and he came by my cell to ask if I wanted to join them. But I had no interest in getting involved, particularly with something like this. I'd already learned my valuable lesson about what can go wrong when you consent to the will of others, so I declined the offer. I sensed that their real aim was to impress some of the more influential players on the wing.

Although Osman was visibly intimidated and rarely left his cell doorway, his timidity would not save him. Nor would the staff, who knew he was a potential target but didn't seem overly concerned. Barely a few weeks after he arrived, the alarms were sounding off as black smoke billowed from his cell. With Osman rarely moving from the officers' view, he made himself a difficult target for a physical attack, and so his cell had been burnt out instead, which takes a matter of seconds to accomplish.

With other prisoners with terrorist convictions beginning to arrive, smoke-filled landings from cell burnouts became a common spectacle on G Wing. During one incident that happened on the 4s landing which has a low ceiling, the fire had been smouldering unnoticed for so long that when the smoke eventually spilled out after someone opened the cell door, it did so with such intensity that it was impossible to see or breathe unless you dropped to your knees and crawled across the floor to the fire exit.

I thought about Danny sometimes. About how a twenty-year friendship could just come crashing to a halt. The experience had scarred me, left me unable to trust other people. And the prison system probably wasn't the best place to attempt to work on rekindling that trust.

With all the time I'd had to reflect, I'd become sceptical about group mentality too. When I was in a group of men full of bravado, I found myself shying away from it – making my excuses and leaving. It wasn't so long ago that I'd have been right at the centre, drawn to it like a magnet, but not now. *I know where these things can lead to,* I'd think to myself. If my predicament wasn't proof of what can go wrong when you exchange some of your individuality for unhealthy group influences, then what is?

Having been at Frankland for a little while by now, I'd become used to the reduced visits as well. My family were only able to visit every couple of weeks, and I became conscious that it was a long way to travel for them and my sisters had families of their own to attend to. I didn't want to be a burden and, at the same time, I could feel the walls going up. My family always made the effort, which I am eternally grateful for, but I knew that part of the way to get through my sentence was to go it alone.

It was easy to see how isolated you can become in prison, not only from society but within prison life. But no man is an island and it's vital to build and maintain some form of connection if you're going to get through it – for mental reasons as well as practical ones. I'd developed a good friendship with Jez, largely by virtue of our shared interest in education, and I'd been hitting the gym a lot, where I joined another lifer called Colin Gunn in some of his training sessions.

Colin was serving 35 years for conspiracy to murder and had a lot of influence across the cat A prisons. You expect monsters in prison but often those in senior positions in the prison population – just like anyone in a senior position in any walk of life – have strong leadership skills and possess some form of charisma. Colin was no different. He was an incredibly personable, well-mannered person – a calm presence amid the chaos. He used his position wisely at

Frankland and kept a lid on some of the trouble, smoothing things over. If it wasn't for Colin, one of Tion's associates – who'd been placed on the hit list because of the attack on Jez – would have lost an eye.

My general perception of British Islamic terrorists at the time was of disenfranchised street kids with low IQs who were easily led and manipulated. Dhiren Barot put that stereotype to bed.

Barot, who arrived on F Wing in 2007, was serving 40 years for plotting terrorist attacks in the UK and US. Although he had an air of arrogance about him, he was quiet, well-kept and highly intelligent. I only became aware of his presence in IT class because of the phenomenal speed at which he could type. Jez knew Barot from his time at the secure unit inside HMP Belmarsh, so we found ourselves debating with him about British politics when he enrolled on the philosophy course.

Born in India and educated in England, Barot had spent time in Kashmir. He wrote a book called *The Army of Madinah in Kashmir* about his time there, in which he described his involvement with the Mujahideen in their fight against the Indian army, as well as his commitment to Islamic jihad. Later, he became an agent for al-Qaeda and carried out extensive surveillance on major American financial institutions. His conviction was considered to be one of the most significant since 9/11.

Very little, if any, of this information was known to the prisoners at Frankland. To them, Barot was just another target who had already been placed on the hit list. But to many of his brothers filtering into the system, including his seven co-defendants, he was not only known, he was revered by them. Dhiren Barot was their *emir* (leader) in rank and esteem. So when he was attacked, allegedly by Gary Moody and an associate, on 18 July 2007 – a pan of boiling-hot cooking oil poured over his head – it caught the attention of every Islamic terrorist and their adherents in the prison system. Despite a news blackout, the account of his attack spilled across the system.

Barot later asked for the charges against Moody to be dropped, but word was already spreading that Frankland was a hostile place for terrorists and extremists. This incident not only reinforced that rumour, it gave fuel to those who wanted to push an agenda that Frankland was developing into somewhere dark and dangerous, not only for extremists but for all Muslims, a place where they would be targeted with extreme acts of violence for simply adhering to their faith or for the colour of their skin.

There were plenty of frequent transfers of prisoners to and from Frankland. Across the prison system, unmanageable prisoners are routinely ghosted (transferred without warning) to other prisons. It is partly meant to disorientate. But apart from sending some prisoners mad, it has another undesirable effect.

During the summer of 2007, another high-profile prisoner arrived, called Blake Summerville. He was serving 35 years for shooting dead a bouncer and a police officer in 1993. Prior to his conviction in 2006, he was considered to be one of the most dangerous men walking the streets of London. With a reputation for extreme violence, Blake was not only another shark (someone who could act alone), he had the backing of many black and mixed-race prisoners. And his arrival at Frankland meant he had just encroached into the territory of another shark – Zane Patton.

Blake and Zane were said to have become deadly rivals after they had begun fighting over the rights to extort money from a convicted rapist at HMP Long Lartin. There was unsettled business between the two. With G and F Wing exercise yards separated by a fence that prevented them from physically reaching each other, a fight was arranged between the pair at the gym.

Blake turned up with a large gang, but there was apparent confusion over timing. They never got to meet. Not satisfied with that outcome, Blake then placed a hit (a contract) on Zane's head for anyone on G Wing brave enough to take it. It was a deed that would have grave ramifications.

With tensions rising between each camp, Dave Andrews, a friend of Zane Patton, found himself fronting up to Carlo Baily, a prisoner convicted of rape and an associate of Blake, on F Wing. After Dave had called him a 'nonce' from the second-floor landing, Carlo, a powerful man who could bench press well over 200kg, raced upstairs towards him. Expecting a fist fight, Dave raised his hands but, before he knew it, he was picked up by Carlo, spun around, and dumped on his head. As Dave lay unconscious, he was kicked and stamped on by Summerville and another accomplice. The incident saw Summerville and Carlo removed to the segregation unit.

Zane was not impressed. Even less so because Dave, according to Zane, had let a 'fucking nonce' beat him.

'You're a fucking embarrassment,' Zane said to Dave. 'What's the matter with yeh? Yeh fucking dizzy cunt!'

Indeed, Dave was a little light-headed. Had the para-medics not managed to bring him round – three times in total, they told him – he would have been dead.

★

For some people in prison, it's religion that gets them through the time. But for me, it was education. I was making good progress. Before moving on to my English GCSE, I had to do a presentation to the class on evolution. I was hoping Jez was going to pop in but he never arrived, so I was left with a class consisting mostly of Muslim students and a Christian who believed that God created the universe in six days. My task involved reading out my personal description of natural selection and then opening myself up to questions.

'So we all came from monkeys? Is that what you're saying?' said one kid with a smirk.

After pitying me for my ignorance, they collectively informed me that I was 'blind', following up with a customary round of applause. To be fair, it turned out to be a good debate. But I was surprised by their out-and-out dismissal of the most basic scientific truths, especially given that they had all been educated in British schools.

Prison brought me closer to people with religious views and I often found myself debating with them. It gave me new insights and enabled me to develop my reasoning, as I was forced to question my own assumptions about life. I also began to appreciate religion more. I could see what it meant to people.

When I first arrived in prison, I would reject religion outright – though that didn't stop me using it as an excuse to get away from the wing for tea and biscuits in the chapel at HMP Hull. But with prisons containing a higher ratio of believers compared to society overall, I became more courteous. I also became aware of its depth and how it encouraged certain positive behaviours, like fasting, resisting excess and possibly helping to improve mental health.

Dave Andrews, who was still recovering from being unceremoniously dropped on his head, was religious, as was his wife, who would regularly come to visit him. Understandably, most relationships don't last a lengthy stretch in prison, but Dave's wife was waiting for him and I think that shared belief was the main driver for that.

I could see how religion offered inmates guidance, structure, a way to conduct themselves. It offered them discipline, perspective – even hope. But I could never spend too long on the topic without a glaring contradiction jumping out at me. After hearing someone espouse the qualities of their beliefs, I'd watch this same person engage in drug dealing, bullying or other supposedly forbidden behaviours. It was clear they were choosing which aspects to follow and which to reject. As far as I could tell, religion was not, as they would claim, compelling them to live better lives.

With many hours spent behind the door in prisons like Frankland, there's a lot of time to think. With an unsettled mind, extended periods of time sealed inside an inescapable box can be extremely corrosive. Abuse, neglect and all manner of traumatic childhood experiences are etched inside the memories of many prisoners. Not the sort of stuff to be ruminated on. But that's exactly what happens if it's not processed properly. Eventually, it can twist the mind into bitterness, leading to resentment towards the state, the prison system and other prisoners. Even towards yourself, which can lead to depression, self-harm, drugs to blot out the thoughts, and even suicide. It's an easy state to fall into and sometimes impossible to climb out of.

For me, my mind leaned towards regret and a degree of self-loathing, but also confusion. In the first two years of my sentence, I yearned to be back on the estate where I grew up. I would spend hours reflecting on my past. Sometimes I'd visualise different trajectories, ones that ended far less destructively, or try to imagine what life might have been like had I not made such stupid mistakes. It haunted me because I could see that just a simple decision here or there could have prevented so much. Of course, it went beyond simple decisions. I'd been so consumed by my lifestyle that I could barely see beyond the pub walls of The Viking. But the further away I drew from that world, the more my perspective changed. Just like planet Earth when you see an image of it from space. The more distant Earth's image, the more insignificant you realise it is compared to the rest of the universe. Despite the conflicts that were engulfing G Wing, my eyes were finally open and I could see where I needed to be. It felt like a gift, strengthening my determination to succeed.

It turned out that not everyone shared the belief that it was impossible to escape from Frankland. On 15 October 2007, David Bieber, an American who was serving 37 years for killing a police officer in Leeds in 2004, was abruptly removed from the prison after his plot to escape from Frankland by helicopter, via G Wing exercise yard, was foiled. Bieber had spoken to his co-conspirator over the phone when he was hatching his plot, inviting him to 'lay down some ground fire' while hovering over the yard. It turned out that Bieber had been speaking to an undercover reporter. And, for reasons that were never fully understood, on the very same day, Colin Gunn was also removed from the wing by prison security and eventually shipped out.

There was always a sense that if Colin left Frankland, the lid would finally be lifted on the tension that had been building and things would properly go off.

CHAPTER 11

War

'Come here, you,' Zane ordered Samuel, beckoning him over. Zane had noticed Samuel talking to a black prisoner he didn't like. 'You either speak to them or you speak to me, all right? Now fuck off!'

'All right, Zane, no problem, mate,' replied Samuel as he scuttled away with his head down.

All prisons have a hierarchy and Samuel, having slid down over the years from a respected position as a gangster/armed robber into something less praiseworthy, had dropped down the rankings. Dangerousness obviously plays a part in this uncodified system, and somewhere near the top of that order are hitmen. There are various types in the system but some of the most active and easiest to recruit are those with an addiction to drugs. Johnny McDonald, a hitman from Manchester, fitted that description neatly. If the price was right, he was even known to take out friends.

I was informed that Johnny had agreed to take the hit on Zane. Normally, a knife would be used to execute such a deed but even a seasoned hitman like Johnny could not take that risk with Zane. He opted to use hot oil instead. However, I was told that while Johnny was in the process of boiling a pan of oil, he was spotted by an influential friend of Zane's and ordered to 'fuck off'. This friend then let Zane know about his discovery and its wing sponsors. Those who had acted as the middlemen between

Blake Summerville and Johnny McDonald were now in a precarious position. And since Zane had the backing of a large group of predominantly white males, G Wing was primed for a tear-up.

Meanwhile, another convicted terrorist, called Kamel Bourgass, had not long arrived. He had been sentenced to life for killing Special Branch Detective Stephen Oake during a raid in Manchester and handed a separate sentence for his involvement in a terrorist plot involving the poison ricin. Bourgass was an odd character whose stay on G Wing was relatively brief.

While I was waiting in the dinner queue, which extended past Bourgass's cell, I was talking to a lad from Middlesbrough called Barry Dean when he offered Bourgass his biscuits. It was purely because Bourgass was the only other person close to him. But for some reason, Bourgass misread Barry's kind gesture.

'Why you trying to pinch from my cell?' queried Bourgass in broken English.

'I'm not,' replied Barry, looking confused. 'I'm just offering you these biscuits.'

'No, no, you're trying to pinch from my cell.'

CRACK! Bourgass slid down the wall while his knees buckled underneath him, collapsing on the ground. Barry had smashed him in the face with a solid left jab.

After Barry had been dragged off to the segregation unit kicking and screaming, Bourgass was left on the wing to lick his wounds. Still seething over his ill-judged encounter, for some reason he decided to attack Tommy, a quiet, 21-year-old prisoner with whom I'd been training. He had clearly not learned from his previous encounter that politeness betrays very little of a man's capacity for savagery. As

Bourgass launched a sneak attack, Tommy didn't bother wasting his energy by throwing punches. Instead, he grabbed Bourgass by his head and bit a chunk out of his face. Had Bourgass known that Tommy had spent time as a teenager in a cage in Durham prison that once held Charlie Bronson, who used to be known as Britain's most violent prisoner, he might have chosen a different target.

A couple of days later, I was making a bacon sandwich one afternoon when I noticed something unusual out the corner of my eye. Zane Patton was in his usual seat, reading his paper, while eight lads strutted past the kitchen. Their group was made up of several members of a notorious crime gang from Birmingham's black community and a couple of religious extremists. It seemed unusual: they weren't regular visitors to that part of the wing, the landing ruled by Zane. It didn't take long to find out why they were here.

The very moment they reached the cell door opposite Zane, they turned and rushed towards him. Drawing bladed objects, they set about Zane with great ferocity, raining numerous blows on to his head as he jumped to his feet. But unbeknown to his attackers, Zane had already prepared himself. In each hand, specially made for the occasion, was a chunk of a broom handle, palm-width in length and with two six-inch nails pierced through each of them, protruding between his fingers − like miniature Wolverine blades. Though the group had overwhelmed Zane in the first few moments, his fight back had already begun. He began to fire multiple strikes towards his unrelenting attackers.

'You fucking cowards!' he screamed.

Chairs were now being used but Zane maintained his position and returned his fair share of damage to anyone who got too close. Other prisoners emerged from their cells and began to join in too.

I wasn't in Zane's circle. In fact, I'd always had the sense that Zane had taken a disliking to me. I was never the type to toady up to someone and try to ingratiate myself. But the manner of this attack, eight against one, the seeming unfairness of those odds, awoke something in me that I was trying to lay to rest. I could feel my adrenaline rise and the old instinctive urge from the streets of Hull – to join in and back the other lads up – stirring. Truth be told, I felt like knocking one of them out, but thankfully just that momentary pause to think about it was enough to stop me getting involved: my resistance was stronger than my compulsion to act and it felt like I'd passed a test of sorts.

After a ferocious sixty seconds of unrestrained violence, the balance of the fight was shifting towards favouring Zane. Whatever the group had set out to achieve was falling apart and they quickly made a run for it while sending their weapons skidding across the landing in all directions. Like the pawmarks of dogs, traces of blood trailed them as they exited the landing.

While this attack had been under way, a group of around twenty prisoners had heard the commotion from downstairs and rushed to investigate. Piling up the stairs in quick succession, they ran straight into the group of eight assailants, taking them by surprise. A second battle instantly took place. Outnumbered, some of the group were set about with intense violence, stabbed in the face and throat, while others broke free and carried out running battles up and down the landings.

With the alarms sounding, an endless stream of officers began spilling onto the wing and beating back prisoners with their batons. Eventually, the fight was broken up, bringing the situation under control but leaving a hyped-up crowd of prisoners loitering protectively outside Zane's cell. An impasse arose as a large group of officers began surrounding the group.

'Everyone, bang-up – now!' shouted an officer.

'Everyone stay where you are!' ordered Samuel, bouncing onto the landing and determined to defy the instructions of the officers.

Everyone just rolled their eyes, accepted that the fight was over and went behind their doors so the injured could be seen to, leaving Samuel standing there looking rather awkward.

The following day, the governors, to everyone's surprise, let everyone back out for association as normal. With Zane in the segregation unit, it was hoped that things might settle again. If there was ever a time when you could cut the atmosphere with a knife, it was then. This feeling was not lost on the group of eight, either. Outnumbered, cut and bruised and probably regretting their actions, barely ten minutes later they unplugged their TV sets and launched them over the railings, sending them crashing to the ground floor in unison and shattering them to pieces. A loud cheer went up. They wanted out of the prison and everyone was quickly banged up again until their wish was granted.

One of the members of the gang who attacked Zane Patton personified some of the contradictions that made up prison life. Despite this violent attack, he was a practising Muslim with whom I'd been playing chess regularly. In an increasingly divided prison, the ancient game of chess had provided some common ground and I was always happy to play with anyone who could offer me a game.

When I first arrived at Frankland I knew how to play chess, but not with any great level of skill. I can't say it formed much of my day-to-day life in Hull before. But just as I had with my formal education, I'd become a student once again – this time of the game. I started by playing games with some other inmates and began to supplement that by reading books from the library about strategy. Two people were allowed in a cell at once, so we'd sometimes play in a cell, or on the landing. Once you see people playing, it's an opportunity to go over and offer them a game some time – which is exactly what this Muslim inmate had done with me. We'd played a few times – occasionally we'd even had to break off games so he could pray. I knew some people on the wing wouldn't approve of my playing with someone like this but that wasn't the way I was doing my sentence.

I found it hard to reconcile his praying with the violence he'd been a part of – but it shouldn't really have come as any sort of surprise to me. While there were winners and losers in the game of chess, there didn't seem to be any obvious winners in the never-ending cycle of violence at Frankland.

By this time, around twenty known al-Qaeda members and sympathisers were being held at Frankland. One of those was Omar Khyam, who was serving 20 years for plotting to explode a fertiliser bomb in London. After spending time in training camps with the Mujahideen in Pakistan, he later returned to Afghanistan to work for the Taliban and al-Qaeda. Khyam, who was an associate of Dhiren Barot, was a devoted and extremely dangerous member of their cause. Standing at just over five feet tall and skinny, his quiet and timid presence went largely unnoticed as he went about his business on F Wing.

This growing number of Muslim inmates led to another area of tension: food and kitchen facilities. Muslims are forbidden from eating non-halal foods, and there was a constant risk of contamination as several men hunched over the same cooker. Some prisoners did try their best to accommodate each other, but with the arrival of more and more men who held uncompromising religious views, 'squabbles were inevitable'.

To try to address this, prison staff exchanged one of the three kitchen knives with a halal one. The Muslim prisoners were only exercising their rights when claiming their own knife, but since the prison authorities refused to allow more than three knives in circulation at any one time, the majority of G Wing was down a knife. To the prisoners who were left having to cut through meat with plastic knives, it was a big deal.

As a response to this, many of the white British inmates began to defend what they saw as their own homegrown culture, which aroused a sense of purpose within them. When trapped inside a mundane environment like a prison, a sense of purpose can be quite stimulating, especially if you've never felt you had one before. As a result, pork and the traditional English breakfast began to symbolise a subtle, though humorous, notion of resistance, leading to an increase in sales of bacon and pork sausages for the canteen supplier. The prison kitchen became the scene of its very own culture war, which felt lighter in tone than the tensions that were simmering on the wing itself.

Omar Khyam had a habit of blending into the background. Someone would usually have noticed the pan of oil bubbling away in one of the kitchens and alerted people. Not this time. With the pan of hot oil held in his hand, almost full to its brim, Khyam strolled from the kitchen where he'd been cooking and down the stairs. He headed towards a group of white prisoners sitting at a table, who were chatting away and minding their own business. One of these men was Malcolm Cruddas, a convicted armed robber who was due to be released. He didn't notice Khyam walk up behind him.

Raising the pan above Cruddas's head, Khyam, without flinching, poured the entire contents all over him. And once he'd completed his mission, he calmly walked over to a group of prison officers and sat down next to them.

It was understandable why people felt compelled to assist Zane Patton. If they could attack him like that, they could attack anyone. Their response was defensive as much as offensive. But the tensions within the prison were something else. The battle for wing control that had formed in people's minds could not be won through violence, which only exacerbated the situation and placed even the most neutral prisoners at risk. It was also unwinnable through physical force because the authorities controlled the battle-field. Whoever the prison allowed to remain on the wing determined the balance of power. At any given moment, any prisoner could be dispersed across the system and plonked in the centre of Whitemoor, Full Sutton or Long Lartin, places where it was said Islamist groups held greater sway.

As men from other category A prisons continued to drift into Frankland, some of the antagonists involved in the fighting began to question their initial enthusiasm. But it was too late for regrets. The genie was out of its bottle and those who had stoked the fire had created deadly

enemies for themselves. An extremist hit list metaphori-
cally referred to as the 'Black Book' ensured they would
not be forgotten.

It didn't really matter to the convicted terrorists, as they
had long ago committed themselves to a violent cause, and
some were only alive because their bombs had failed to
detonate while strapped to them; nor the hardened gang
members and individuals (on both sides), who made a living
out of reputational violence.

Given that backing down without losing face had its own
risks, many of the white prisoners had left themselves with
little choice but to continue fighting. And this meant that
if a potential rival landed at Frankland, they were faced
with the unenviable task of either having to deal with
him or risk being the target of a sneak attack. They were
effectively trapped in a never-ending cycle of violence.
When you're serving a sentence of 30-plus years, it's not
like you can just pack your bags and leave.

From this period on, any trouble between a Muslim and
non-Muslim prisoner was viewed through the context of
this growing struggle for wing dominance. If there are two
subjects that have the capacity to enflame conflict between
humans, they are race and religion. War with a hint of jihad
was now official. Certain prisoners were not just turning
up to kill off a bit of bird. They were doing so to kill.
After six major incidents occurred in one month alone, as
far as the staff at Frankland was concerned the prison had
just entered the most violent period in its history. As such,
G and F Wings were fitted out with a complex array of
security cameras, including one above every other cell.

It felt like a grim irony that I'd chosen to renounce
violence during the most violent period in the history of

this category A prison, but that was my lot. There are different groups of people in prison – it's an odd mix at times – but I was fortunate to find myself hanging around and sharing meals with a group that included Jez and a couple of other big players. These were people who could look after themselves, so other inmates would think twice about messing with them, but who didn't necessarily want to get involved in any of the trouble on the wings. Trying to stay out of all that – to remain neutral, if you like – was difficult at times and it came with its own risks. Once you say no to getting involved in the trouble, you put yourself in a certain position and have to navigate your way through that. But the promise I'd made to myself meant that these were risks I was willing to take.

As prisoners from diverse backgrounds continued to arrive at Frankland, the atmosphere grew noticeably even more tense. Some inmates even raised the idea of creating separate wings for certain individuals, but with rules in place that prevented the segregation of prisoners based on ethnicity or religion, the prison authorities had little choice but to allow potential rivals to socialise.

Prisoner education and the completion of offending behaviour work are important prison-service objectives, and such aims would be impossible to achieve without allowing prisoners to interact. Most prisoners do, after all, re-enter society. Activities and courses not only allow prisoners to engage in work to address their offending behaviour, but also the opportunities to provide evidence of risk reduction. The downside, of course, is that when prisoners have an opportunity to interact, that always provides a window for the propagation of the very issues that these interventions try to eradicate – ideas and influences that are detrimental to both prisoners and society. But with the growing influx of prisoners who held more extreme views, the risk–reward balance of time out of cell was skewed by a new problematic challenge: the grooming and radicalisation of prisoners.

When you spend years under the same roof as people convicted of terrorism, and extremists, you naturally get to engage in conversations, whether in a dinner queue, at the gym or perhaps in class. You learn all sorts. As in other walks of life, there is variety. Some of these men are not approachable and do not engage at all with prisoners outside their faith, while some are not outwardly violent and are very well presented. Others, such as my occasional chess companion, seek out opportunities to connect over a shared interest. Some are incredibly good communicators, and charismatic. They know their subject very well, or at least their interpretation of it, which typically involves resentment of the British state, thanks to its military intervention in the Middle East, and the inferiority and moral vacuum of Western culture. Yet, the thing is, though they are looking at it through the prism of extremist ideology, some of their grievances have a degree of legitimacy. And the sense of alienation felt by many youths in certain parts of the West is valid. So it's not difficult for groomers to convince someone who has little or no knowledge of history and international affairs that their or the world's problems are entirely the fault of the West. If you can articulate what someone is feeling, you can strike a chord and take advantage of that.

I would often see a newly arrived prisoner fall under the wing of an extremist or gang member. Groomers, who are often charismatic or formidable alpha males, know that when a new arrival enters a prison like Frankland, they are likely to be scared, directionless, impressionable and possibly resentful towards the justice system. The target is treated with kindness, offered nice food and brought into a welcoming circle of friends. At a moment of loneliness and despair in your life, that's comforting. Then they are exposed to a set of values that set them apart from the prison population. At a time when you are confused about your own life, that's intriguing and perhaps enlightening. Then they are offered a reason for their existence, reinforced with literature and an ideology. Now that's a sense of purpose with meaning. And anyone who converts to Islam receives an Arabic name – a new identity to separate them from their culture, their past and, quite possibly, their family.

And it can happen fast. New arrivals are often very approachable, but after spending time in the wrong company, they tend to stop engaging more generally. A new guy might make the effort to chat to everyone but gradually the signs start: he's hanging around with the extremists more, chatting to the other prisoners less. And once that change in demeanour is picked up by prisoners who don't share the same views, the new guy is then perceived as a potential threat. If only subtly at first, they behave differently towards the convert, which, in turn, reinforces the guidance he is receiving from his groomers: don't trust anyone but us.

Freedom of religious practice is protected by law in Britain. In prisons, however, this law has found itself being wielded far more deftly. Clued-up extremists know that the right to religious practice makes it harder for the prison authorities to intervene when they groom other prisoners and disseminate their ideology, behaviours they can easily pass off as sharing or debating one's faith. In practice, allowing convicted terrorists and extremists to

associate with other prisoners makes grooming very difficult to prevent.

But it is not half as difficult to spot. Going from being
clean shaven and wearing a Nike tracksuit to suddenly
wearing a kameez and sporting a long beard is one possible
sign. Sure, appearance is not everything. And being able to
differentiate between genuine faith and religious extremism
is essential if you want to avoid marginalising people and
giving fuel to the wrong people. Nor does the process
of radicalisation require the presence of a spiritual aspect.
But inferences can often be made from the type of prisoner someone is spending time with – like, for example,
a convicted terrorist.

It is possible that most of the prisoners I saw fall into
the arms of extremists were playing along, just looking
for protection or companionship to see them through the
darkest days of their sentence or until their eventual release.
I have a hunch that many will leave prison and probably
never pray or read the Quran again. But some won't.

CHAPTER 12

Extreme Problem, Extreme Solutions

While the issues at Frankland had been bubbling away, so too had my application to the Court of Appeal. I had still never fully understood why the alternative verdict of manslaughter had not been open to me at my trial and I wanted to pursue this, along with another technical issue that arose following my conviction.

To be clear, I knew I wasn't going home, no matter what. I had played my part in that man's death and was rightly serving punishment for it – I wasn't in denial – but I held out an unlikely hope for eight to ten years for manslaughter rather than a life sentence. The major difference between the two is that with the former you're guaranteed to get out after a certain time, whereas with the latter you're not guaranteed to get out at all.

I knew I wasn't going to go back to how I was before and if there was the opportunity to possibly get some time off my sentence, to lessen its impact, then why wouldn't I at least try? It's human nature to want to at least attempt these things and I would come to learn how important these opportunities are to all prisoners: not just appeals but anything that might offer the chance to reduce the length of a sentence, even by a matter of months or a year or two. Because they helped fuel that crucial yet most difficult thing to maintain in prison: hope.

On 12 May 2008, I was taken by prison bus to HMP Brixton in London. I was not required to attend the appeal court in person but, given the issues on the wing, I thought it would make for a much-needed change of scenery. Prior to my hearing, I was escorted through a protracted set of narrow passageways to a room where my new Queen's Counsel was waiting. We shook hands and sat down.

'I've already spoken to Mr Campbell. We are not going to bear fruit today,' explained my counsel in a sombre tone.

Appeal dismissed! The court had explained that unless it could be proven that Danny and I had acted together, there were no grounds for a conviction for either murder or manslaughter, as the medical evidence did not support the idea that only some of the injuries had been fatal. Therefore, the trial judge had correctly directed the jury on joint enterprise and was not required to leave the option of manslaughter on the indictment.

That was it: done. Within a matter of days, I was back in a sweat box enduring the five-hour return trip to Frankland, still carrying the label 'murderer'. And with my appeal now dismissed, it was a label I was going to have to get used to. I'd taken the law into my own hands, used violence and someone lost their life.

In April 2005, the month I was arrested, a new sentence called Imprisonment for Public Protection (IPP) was brought into law via the Criminal Justice Act. IPP sentences were intended for repeat dangerous offenders and had a life span of 99 years. Like a life sentence, they came with a minimum term (tariff), the minimum length of time the recipient would have to spend in prison before being allowed to apply for release through the Parole Board.

IPPs and life sentences are called indeterminate sentences, as they have no natural end, unlike determinate sentences, which have a fixed release date. Any indeterminate sentence prisoner could spend the rest of their life in prison if they fail to convince the Parole Board that their detention is no longer neccessary for public protection. By mid-summer 2008, the prison system had become littered with IPP prisoners and Frankland had received its fair share.

Because of the media hype surrounding this type of sentence, some prisoners initially carried the IPP label with pride. Two such prisoners were Birchy and Johnno, who had been so keen to make an example of Hussain Osman when he arrived at Frankland. Now that it had dawned on them that their names had been etched firmly into the pages of the Black Book and one of their sidekicks had been transferred to Whitemoor prison, they sought to bolster their numbers.

'We're all vulnerable,' Birchy warned me in the kitchen one day. 'You in or what?'

He had a point. But I could find myself being at Frankland a long time and I had no ambitions to get my name on a hit list. I wanted to avoid any form of conflict but I was beginning to understand that even the act of remaining neutral was a choice in itself that could have consequences.

Then again, no one was more vulnerable than him, the person who'd helped stir the hornet's nest, because he was over tariff, which meant he had served his minimum term and was eligible for a parole hearing and could, unlike others, more quickly escape the mess.

'No, thanks,' I replied.

Birchy, who was not my friend and would not assist me if I was in trouble, walked off in a huff.

★

Jez and I had got to know a couple of Muslim prisoners who offered to cook us tandoori chicken. It was one of the best meals we'd ever had in prison, so we asked them to show us how to cook it. We never did achieve their standards but tandoori chicken became a regular meal choice of ours. Like Jez, who was mixed race, I didn't judge someone on their ethnic background or philosophy on life. So long as they weren't contributing towards the violence and division in the prison, we treated them with respect.

But not everyone shared that view. The ongoing tensions on the wing were beginning to create an oppressive atmosphere even for Muslim prisoners who had nothing to do with the troubles. Khyam's hit on Cruddas had certainly made people more anxious about sneak attacks and showed that meekness meant little where someone's ability to cause serious injury was concerned.

While the anxiety was understandable, one of the methods of addressing it wasn't. The two prisoners who'd cooked for me and Jez had been at Frankland for years and never troubled anyone, yet their names had been placed on the hit list. In other words, they were 'getting it' courtesy of Birchy and some of his associates.

From my position on the balcony I watched Birchy's gang coordinate their ranks. A brief shift in the power balance on the wing meant there was a window of opportunity to strike, so the pressure was on. But it just didn't sit right with me that these two prisoners were about to be the target of extreme violence for little more than appearing different – or because power, through strength in numbers, had fleetingly come into the hands of one group.

Strength, I'd come to appreciate, can also mean resisting the urge to respond with aggression or the pressure of your peers, even when you're scared. Throughout this hostile period at Frankland, I'd been reading about the historical fight against oppression and intolerance in philosophy class. In one way, it gave me an intellectual framework through which to understand what was happening on the wing, while in another it was like I had a window into another time, allowing me to empathise with long-dead people living under oppression.

I was also able to better understand the ethical perspectives of those I studied. I could appreciate how injustice had helped develop their ideas and understood why violence and oppression had compelled certain individuals throughout history to take great personal risks on behalf of others. Rather than use violence to defeat violence, the people I studied had used their intellect to fight injustice, actions which eventually pulled humanity into a more enlightened episode of our history, where reason, ethics and better laws empowered the weak to resist the strong. In many ways, it felt like I'd found role models in the literature, a way to extract light from the dark energy that was growing across the system and ease my journey towards my ultimate goal.

The chivs were being sharpened, the hit was on. It was not our place to forewarn the two Muslim prisoners of their fate. But when I heard one of the gang talking quite loudly and openly about the hit, I felt something stir in me. I turned round and told him what I thought.

'It's bullying,' I said.

The person on the receiving end was not happy about it at all. He just looked at me. The atmosphere turned tense in a way that it wasn't before, despite the impending hit.

But there were no direct repercussions. Not then, anyway. Time would tell if I'd landed myself in trouble further down the line.

Thankfully, the two Muslim prisoners, despite being moments from being lynched, were spared at the last moment. The hit was called off. I never found out why – and I had no intention of asking, either.

The oppressive atmosphere at Frankland created a climate of fear, which can be another driver of violence. Some prisoners would turn up with one goal in mind – strike, draw blood, get sent to the seg unit then let the authorities quickly transfer them to another establishment. Given the potential for it to result in a serious charge it was a risky tactic, but with rumours rife across the system about Frankland's hostility towards prisoners convicted of terror offences, it must have seemed like the lesser of two evils.

The only place to escape physical violence for those tangled up in the politics of prison life was the segregation unit. But it's a pretty extreme solution. Not only are they depressing and uncomfortable places, with a concentration of nutcases and staff who don't really want you there, long-term isolation can cause psychological damage. And you also run the risk of being labelled a 'grass' or shunned by your own, making any transition back to the wing even harder. At some point, you will have to leave and either face your own or a growing enemy.

I thought back to my only stint in a seg unit, back in HMP Hull, with Robby my next-door neighbour. It made me think how far I'd come in a relatively short space of time, to have been able to exercise enough self-control not to repeat the verbal violence that had landed me in

Hull's subterranean dungeon, let alone to have engaged in any physical violence that could have landed me in further hot water. I had no wish to visit Frankland's seg unit but what had changed in me to make this possible?

My last stint in a seg unit had been because of my reaction to Jayne being told to keep her hands off me, just as my last act of physical violence had, at least in my mind, been motivated as an act of revenge for an attack on Jayne, a violation of our home. I was well aware now that Jayne had not wanted me to react, that revenge in the way I envisaged it was the last thing she'd needed. With Jayne no longer in my life, those strong emotions she inspired in me were no longer being stirred, and without my mates inside, that pack mentality, spurring me on to act in ways my friends would approve of, was no longer there.

But it was more than that. The vices I'd traded – the drink, drugs, cigarettes exchanged for education, chess, the gym – had brought me clarity, a feeling of self-possession. I alone was responsible for my actions – not Jayne, not Danny or my mates. I had shown that I could steer clear of trouble, could go my own way even when the herd was going in the opposite direction. I had proven I could achieve something measurable too. I now had some GCSEs, including in English. While this might be the kind of accomplishment many take for granted, I had gone from being a man who left school with no qualifications to gaining some in a relatively short space of time. Next up, A level philosophy, a subject that had inspired me and gripped my imagination.

It was just as well that I had no designs whatsoever on Frankland's seg unit. The prison began running out of cell spaces there. But it was not necessarily filling up for punishment purposes – it was with men who were too fearful to remain on G or F Wings. In response, the prison closed a whole landing on G Wing (the 4s landing, which consisted of 25 cells), so that they could accommodate prisoners who were unwilling to return to their normal location. In all but name, it became a vulnerable prisoner unit.

Creating this unit inevitably meant that a contingent of men had to be relocated to F Wing, next door. Over that same period, a number of convicted terrorists and their sympathisers also landed on F wing.

'You'll never guess what I've just seen,' said a prisoner as he walked onto G Wing. 'You couldn't make it up.'

He led me to where we could see the exercise yard. Men would often do extra fitness sessions in the yard but this was the first time anyone had seen a group of prisoners performing army crawls on its concrete surface. Discretion, it seemed, was out of fashion.

F Wing was on edge in any case after an extremist had been heard saying, 'As soon as more brothers arrive, we can take over.'

This comment didn't go down well and, in July 2008, Kamel Bourgass – who'd been removed from G Wing following his unlucky encounters with two northern hard-cases – had his cell burnt out. Shortly after, an extremist retaliated by slicing a prisoner across his face. This attack instantly led to a fight between opposing sides, resulting in several Muslim prisoners being seriously injured. As staff tried to intervene, they too were set about as F Wing descended into a riot.

With my cell facing the front entrance to F Wing, I had box seats. I watched from my window while a continuous stream of around one hundred and fifty prison officers piled onto F Wing to join the fray. Wave after wave of prison officers went in, kitted out with batons and shields. What first struck me was an odd observation: *I never realised how many people worked in this prison.* It was a thought quickly subsumed by the cacophony of over two hundred men shouting, screaming, banging and fighting on F Wing. It was a wild, unsettling noise, amplified by the unique acoustics of the prison, that seemed to travel right through me and go on for ever. (In reality, it was probably over in about twenty minutes.) As the noise peaked at its crescendo and then slowly came down, the last of the resistance was quashed and the consequences gradually became clear. A large number of prisoners had suffered injuries, as well as four officers, including one whose arm had been broken.

As I took in the aftermath of the carnage, I was thankful not to have been a part of it. The primal, violent sound of it is something I will never forget. It occurred to me then that there was something else at play in my efforts to turn my back on violence, beyond my new sense of responsibility and the cessation of my vices: the element of luck. I was lucky that riot hadn't happened on G Wing, that I hadn't been caught in the middle of it. It was a reminder that, for all the control I was now asserting over my own life and actions, circumstances could still put me in a position where the choice about whether to use violence again might not be just mine to make.

There was another solution to the violence and fear that was now spreading across the prison system, one that seemingly no longer simply required a period of grooming, but which was being done wilfully and opportunistically: converting to Islam. In the Quran, it says it is not permissible to harm a fellow Muslim and this principle was now being used by extremist prisoners to help bolster their ranks, a tactic that had already proved useful at other dispersal prisons.

Of course, it's anyone's right to join the spiritual ranks of a religion if they so choose, and prisoners converting to Islam was not a new phenomenon in British prisons. But the motivation for some certainly was. For some converts, especially those with a taste for violence, the primary incentive was membership of the most powerful gang emerging across category As, while for others it was driven by intimidation and the fear of retaliatory violence. In certain cases, basic human needs like safety and belonging were being sold to the highest bidders.

It was an opportunity that was actively marketed to any prisoner convicted of any crime, even child killers. Once someone converts, every deed of the past is erased, no matter how depraved. With all previous sins cleansed, it makes it far easier to accept someone who, for instance, has raped a woman or murdered a child.

Traditionally, men serving time for rape or offences against children were given a hard time and often subjected to violence if they had not sought sanctuary on a safe wing. So this doorway to a relative safe zone must have been music to the ears of those who had always been seen by the general prison population as repulsive and inferior. Almost overnight, the long-established pecking order was flipped on its head as any converted sex offenders became more or less untouchable. After years of being at the bottom of the pile, some were now walking around with a strut and beginning to join in on the violence inflicted on the infidels.

★

You meet some very clever men in prison and some natural leaders, but they have usually plied their trade through violence in one form or another. Negotiating peace treaties is rarely part of their repertoire. Which is a shame, because with these skills available it might have been possible to avoid some of the division and violence that erupted during that time.

The lack of leadership from the prison managers was also evident by its absence. Throughout my time at Frankland, not once did I see the governor or his SLT (senior leadership team) on the wing, nor did they attempt to mediate in what was so obviously developing into an intractable conflict with grave implications. If the televised conflicts in the Middle East were not enough to demonstrate what can go wrong when tensions involving ethnicity and religion flare up, then I don't know what is.

At best, cameras were installed and people were removed from the wing only after an incident had occurred. Considering the high-security approach is heavily centred around responsive rather than pre-emptive interventions, mediating on behalf of dangerous prisoners is not a natural part of its make-up. Which is another shame in this context because what was happening at Frankland not only enabled the development of increasingly extreme positions in the mindsets of some of its white population, but it helped to strengthen the radical Islamist pretext that they were right while the ideas of the infidel were wrong.

As part of my sentence, I needed to do a violence-reduction course, which, perhaps ironically, wasn't available in category A Frankland. So I'd put in an application to HMP Gartree, a category B prison in Leicestershire, where the course was available. The powers that be looked at my record and said, 'Look, you've been doing really well, we're going to let you move.'

This was an important moment for me. It offered a huge amount of positive reinforcement to the way I'd been conducting myself, showing me that if I stayed on this path, progress was possible. Perhaps most crucially of all, it was the first moment of my sentence that offered tangible hope.

Progressing like this through the system was my aim and my behaviour was of course crucial to it. The reason people like Zane Patton and Blake Summerville had remained category A prisoners for years was because of their behaviour inside: moving someone like them to a category B prison just wouldn't be possible, as it wouldn't have the sort of security required to manage them. But for those of us of a more even temperament in Frankland, the aim was to progress from category A to B, then to C and eventually down to category D towards the end of our tariff, which is the open prison environment, where we would have a better chance of applying for parole and getting it. In effect, you have to prove yourself at each level, ticking off numerous boxes along the way, before you can apply for release.

In barely two and a half years at Frankland I'd witnessed huge change in the culture of the prison. At times it was dark and intimidating, but it was also enlightening in the sense that it accelerated my own journey on the road to a better place. Though my past had hung over me, as I observed a competition of hate, fear and confusion going on around me, it had motivated me, reinforcing my growing disillusionment with violence and antisocial behaviour. Never before had the folly of violence as a solution to any problem been made so clear to me, especially once

I saw it being committed in a seemingly never-ending cycle that solved nothing, only increased the problems for individuals and the prison at large.

My time at HMP Frankland had allowed me to begin to better understand how people can be shaped and influenced by their surroundings and circumstances. The men I observed were not born bad people. They were, at least mostly, imprisoned not only by the cell walls around us but by their minds, just as I had been for most of my life. I was now able to recognise that part of my world had been made up of self-defeating ideas – ideas that I'd been too content with.

Despite the many years I had left to serve, my mind was beginning to work its way loose from the shackles that had prevented me from being myself. And while I was determined to one day achieve my freedom, what was keeping me going in the meantime was developing this deep sense of purpose I had begun to build. In an environment such as a prison, where you're serving a life sentence, a purpose can be a powerful thing.

I still had much to learn but there were glimmers of light ahead in the tunnel as I prepared to leave Frankland. After saying goodbye to Jez, for what would turn out to be the last time, I loaded my belongings onto a trolley and set off on the long walk towards Frankland's reception. While passing the prison library, I noticed some flower beds. The natural colours, non-existent in and around G and F Wings, immediately caught my visual senses. I'd been starved of colours like this – I couldn't remember the last time I'd set eyes on something as simple as a flower. It struck me then that we all need a bit of colour in our lives.

PART IV

Category B: HMP Gartree

CHAPTER 13

A Room with a View

I arrived in HMP Gartree in February 2009. After the madness of Frankland, I found Gartree, a category B prison that holds just over 700 men, mostly on life sentences, very laid-back. Its relatively calm atmosphere meant prisoners could worry less about the threat of violence from each other and focus more on personal development and completing offending behaviour work. Lifers who have served many years of their sentence know how to do their jail.

At Gartree, men could also mix freely with each other, with no separate wings for prisoners based on offence. Men convicted for crimes that would normally be looked down upon lived relatively peacefully among the other prisoners, something that is unthinkable at many other prisons. Although there were no known sex offenders at Gartree, it did contain men who'd been convicted of killing a close relation, like a partner, a friend or their child. This is why Gartree had an offending behaviour course called 'Healthy Relationships'. In prison lingo, these men were referred to as 'Domestics'.

Gartree had a large psychology department that ran several OBPs (offending behaviour courses), which were essential for reducing a prisoner's risk and enabling them to move towards release one day. The relationship between inmates and the prison staff felt a bit better at Gartree too. At Frankland, you didn't want to spend too long talking to the staff because it might look suspicious in some people's eyes, but here things were a bit more relaxed and the divide was less marked than where I'd come from.

The prison was ideal because it allowed me to burn off a few years in a relatively peaceful environment and get the all-important psychology work concluded. My risk level was high, partly because of my youth offending, and if I wasn't able to reduce it, I wouldn't be able to progress through the system.

Following conviction, prisoners are assessed through a tool called OASys (Offender Assessment System) by probation officers who identify factors that contribute to offending. The OASys tool then provides a number of scores which indicate the likelihood of someone reoffending on release from prison. It is these 'risk' factors that prisoners are encouraged to work on and ultimately reduce their risk to the public, as well as each other and themselves if necessary.

One of my risk factors was related to emotional control. My anger, or at least my poor control of it, played its part in clouding my judgement on the night that I approached my victim. Other risk factors of mine related to my lifestyle choices, for example, my misuse of substances. Having these in black and white meant I was able to focus on addressing them. And by working on these factors, it meant that when it came time to potentially move on, say, to a category C prison down the line, there would be fewer reasons to say no to me. By the same token, it would be almost impossible for me to receive permission to move on from the prison without first addressing these risk factors through the available courses, or at least being assessed by a psychologist as unsuitable.

All this information, including personal data, offence type, intelligence on your wing behaviour and positive factors like your educational achievements, is held on a central-ised system called PNOMIS (Prison National Offender Management System) that can be accessed by professionals across the system at different levels appropriate to their role.

I'd never really been a goals-orientated person before but this road map to progress through the prison system offered me goals in my life for the first time. It presented a way forward, a route to stick to, which required me not to succumb to any temptations that might steer me away from this path. I was determined to keep to it – to be so disciplined about achieving something it offered me an alluring sense of purpose and meaning. This level of discipline too was new to me. Yes, I'd worked and held down jobs before I was inside, but I would often be late to work, hungover, and I was bad with money, which I'd often blow at the weekend on going out. But being inside and having something to work towards offered me a focus I'd never felt so keenly before.

I immediately jumped back into education too, and I became a learning support assistant in ICT and then later a peer mentor on the substance misuse course. I continued to accrue more qualifications, particularly anything to do with computers, which I'd never really used before prison and which I was determined to become as proficient with as possible. With my renewed sense of purpose, my focus was geared towards developing myself in any way I could.

I soon made friends with Gaz, a Yorkshire lad who'd just received a life sentence with a minimum tariff of 33 years. He had been part of a group who had attempted to extract money from an apparent drug dealer, but some of them went beyond what was originally planned. What started out as a burglary ended up as a murder. Any murder conviction involving 'gain' carries a sentence starting point of 30 years. Despite the separate roles played, the law of joint enterprise held everyone collectively responsible for the victim's death. It was Gaz's first offence.

Gaz's sentence, which was the longest in Gartree at the time, typified a new era of sentence increases that altered the standard that British criminals had become used to. Tony Blair's mantra 'Tough on crime, tough on the causes of crime' ended the days when criminals could expect between 12 and 15 years for taking someone's life. It certainly put my sentence into perspective. I could say, 'I've *only* got thirteen and a half years left,' and somehow mean it. 25 and 35 year recommendations were now the new norm. With sentences of this length, you might well end up dying inside. You're certainly going to be old if you ever do get out. How do you even begin to go about rationalising a route through the system in these sorts of time frames?

It may have cut a few politicians some slack but the length of these new sentences was bound to have knock-on effects. When sentences start to clear the 20-year mark, they tend to reduce hope. And if there is one thing that has the ability to disrupt prison regimes, it's when prisoners cannot envisage their future. I was lucky in some ways that I had this potential end point to aim for. But for Gaz and the increasing number of people entering the system with these sentences around their necks, what did they have to aim for?

★

It didn't take long before Gaz and I moved over to C Wing, which was much more settled than the constant comings and goings on the induction wing. After seeing nothing but drab prison structures for the last few years, this time I got lucky and could see what lay beyond the prison fence. I had landed a cell that overlooked a vast stretch of rolling countryside, where the odd hot-air balloon drifted past and paragliders swirled in the air currents overhead.

'What would you be doing out there now, Gaz?' I asked, immediately regretting it, as I'd forgotten for a moment how long he was serving.

Some prisoners don't like a view. It tortures them and they prefer to face inwards. But a view inspired me and I would often sit for long periods looking out across the fields, watching the wildlife and contemplating my future and freedom. I always felt that keeping one eye focused on life beyond prison was important to retaining some hope, maintaining my mental health and achieving my ultimate goal, which was of course my eventual release.

Sport and fitness had also begun to play a more serious role in my life. If I wasn't weightlifting or running, I'd be playing volleyball, badminton or anything else that came my way. Gaz and I also began doing cell workouts, hitting pads after an officer lent us his boxing gloves, and learning Brazilian jiu-jitsu.

Coming from rugby towns, Gaz and I were both passionate about the sport, so we persuaded the gym staff to put rugby league on the PE timetable. Full contact was banned but once we mustered enough men to join us, our games could still get fairly heated, which is not surprising given that practically everyone was serving a life sentence for murder.

To avoid getting stuck at Gartree, one of my priorities was to complete a violence reduction course. But time was beginning to pass. My place on the waiting list had remained static because Gartree held a growing number of IPP prisoners who were now starting to exceed their tariff expiry dates. Due to having short tariffs on paper, they were being prioritised over mandatory life sentence prisoners for offending behaviour courses. The problem with the IPP sentence was that it required the Parole Board to direct release, but with IPP minimum tariffs being relatively short compared to mandatory life sentence tariffs like mine, IPP prisoners were unable to get onto courses that would help them reduce their risk levels in time for their on-tariff parole hearings. The lack of funding for these courses meant there were simply too few places available, leading to a national backlog that was clogging up the whole system.

When the IPP was initially passed into law, it was expected that around 900 men would receive the sentence. Instead, it rapidly shot up to 8,000. With so many men over tariff and with no reasonable prospect of release anytime soon, the justice secretary Ken Clarke would eventually abolish them in 2012, but the Act didn't take effect retro-spectively, leaving 6,000 men imprisoned for a sentence that no longer existed, and leading Ken Clarke to later remark that the IPP sentence had become a 'stain on the justice system'.

With so many IPPs already beyond their tariff expiry dates, the indeterminate aspect of the sentence made it conceivable, certainly to those who had complex needs or were impulsive, that they might never be released. At a time when the prison system was about to take another turn for the worse, the last thing it needed was an additional group of men who lacked hope impacting resources and the prison environment.

Though I remained on the waiting list for the violence reduction course, I was fortunate that Gartree was one of few prisons to facilitate CALM (Controlling Anger and Learning to Manage it), an offending behaviour course that actually covered any type of emotion and how to manage it. Offending behaviour courses usually involve keeping daily logs of challenging experiences and your thought processes so that facilitators can provide you with the relevant skills and write progress reports.

After I completed the CALM course, I began to notice more acutely the advantages of emotional control in various aspects of life. I came across a story about a hostage nego-tiator who was very adept at controlling his emotions, an invaluable attribute for that line of work. But since emotions can influence our judgement without us neces-sarily realising, during a hostage negotiation he would have someone monitor him and tap him on the shoulder if he showed any signs of emotion.

In the prison environment, there is a seemingly never-ending supply of experiences challenging to your thinking. There are myriad opportunities for frustration. Like you're hungry and you go down for something to eat but the food looks terrible. *What the fuck is this shit?* People kick off all the time at the servery. Or it might be that you're queuing up with a load of guys to go to the gym and all of a sudden the alarm goes off – there's a fight on another wing, who knows what the cause is – and everything is locked down until it's resolved. So all of a sudden you can't go to the gym – and remember this means missing out or deferring what is a really important part of your day, most of which has been monotonous and frustrating. How are you dealing with this? Some prisoners get frustrated and can't control themselves. 'Fucking hell . . .' they might suddenly blurt out and start having a go at the prison officers.

So by keeping these logs as part of the CALM course, I was demonstrating that I was using the correct skills that I'd been taught to help me manage challenging situations, because they can be incredibly frustrating. For example, I might decide to use self-talk to cope. *It's OK. It's not a problem,* I might say. *There's always tomorrow.*

It can be utterly tedious, of course, monitoring and making notes of your thoughts and how you're responding to situations you wouldn't normally think twice about. But without a doubt, in addition to easing and possibly speeding up your journey through your sentence thanks to a favourable report, they offer very useful insights into your own thinking and behaviour and bring you more in tune with who you are at a more fundamental level.

Prisons are a great test of emotions. Men with predatory traits and mental health issues challenge each other daily. Someone walks past and knocks into you, someone ignores you or won't get out of your way on the stairs. How are you dealing with that? People do all sorts of weird things – someone might take a shit in the shower. Or someone might be blasting music at a ridiculous volume out of their cell when you're trying to have a bit of down time. And these are just the little challenges – piled on top of the bigger issues like violence, drugs and gangs. Week in, week out, and for years on end.

And then there are the prison conditions. Freezing cold in winter and yet a sweatbox in the summer, it's enough to push some already very unhinged people over the edge.

In our cells in the summer, we would often put our feet in cold water and ice just to try to keep cool, while in winter I would often get into my bed wearing a coat and hat just to keep warm. The heating systems were old and unreliable, and on some days when there was no hot water for the showers, it could be a real challenge.

'If you can get through this in one piece, you deserve a fucking medal,' I'd often hear prisoners say.

Things went well over the first year or so, but reminders of the violence that I'd left behind were never far away. Like during this time, Barry Dean arrived. Barry was the prisoner who'd punched Kamel Bourgass in the face after he'd accused him of pinching from his cell. After becoming embroiled in further incidents at Frankland, he was transferred to Long Lartin, a high-security category A prison that was largely under the control of the Islamist terrorist group.

When he arrived at Lartin, a reception officer who was reading through Barry's file looked him in the eyes and asked inquisitively, 'You got any problems here?'

Barry knew full well his name had been engraved into the pages of the Black Book but shook his head. 'No,' he replied.

When Barry walked onto the wing, he felt the atmosphere change as loitering groups of prisoners turned to eyeball the new arrival. He knew it was just a matter of time. Ten minutes, it turned out.

'Where've you come from mate?' asked a black guy.

'Frankland,' he replied.

Barry only found out what had happened to him because an officer gave him the rundown when he woke up.

While the prisoner had drawn him into a conversation, around ten others sneaked up from behind and attacked him with an assortment of makeshift weapons. Barry was lucky not to have been blinded. With stab marks circling his eyes, his attackers had obviously attempted to remove them, but failed as they fell over each other in the passion of the assault.

CHAPTER 14

The *Daily Mail* Test

The prison system's bureaucratic processes can be just as testing as anything another inmate has to offer. This bureaucracy often delays even the simplest of tasks and reduces accountability for decision makers. It can be extremely disheartening, especially if a rule has been imposed by politicians whose chief concern is to be perceived as being tough on criminals, rather than having rehabilitation as its motivation. Very little of note is carried out in collaboration with the prisoners, the people who know their environment better than anyone.

It was the new governor, Ian Telfor, who decided to do something about this. Telfor arrived at Gartree in 2012 and one of his first acts was to set up a Prisoner Council, an innovative and very effective way to give prisoners a voice. Having spent the previous six years in education departments, I was given an ideal opportunity to start applying some of my knowledge – though it wasn't as simple as volunteering. Just like regional councillors, candidates would have to get voted in. For interested prisoners, this meant writing a manifesto, canvassing for votes and attending a husting.

Turning up to a packed multi-faith centre with my manifesto and the slogan 'Tough on bureaucracy, tough on the causes of bureaucracy' was certainly different to what I had been used to, but I knew I could only grow by throwing myself in at the deep end. With these things largely a popularity contest, I soon found myself on Gartree's first Prisoner Council along with six others.

While elections at Gartree had been under way, a more powerful political shift had been occurring at national level. In September 2012, the Conservative MP Chris Grayling was promoted to the role of Justice Secretary. From press coverage of his appointment, it was clear he was going to take a hostile approach, the extent of which few could have predicted.

With hindsight, it's quite possible Governor Telfor had been warned about the changes to come. He gave us a great deal of autonomy with the council and on our suggestion made our roles full-time, with full pay of £25 per week. A friend of mine called Daz, a natural public speaker who could address a packed stadium without breaking into a sweat, became the chair and Mark, another friend, became the vice-chair. Mark didn't have a street-wise bone in his body but, having previously worked for IBM, he had some very useful IT skills. He built a database to log and track every issue raised and provide statistical feedback on each councillor's progress, as well as, to their irritation, the prison's senior leadership team. Each wing was supplied with the minutes of every meeting and kept fully updated on all our proposals. We set about building and running Gartree's Prisoner Council with such energy and proficiency that Governor Telfor could not believe what he'd unleashed. He later confessed, 'You lot scared me at first.'

And Telfor was not easy to scare. He was a governor who led from the front. You knew where you stood with him and his sense of direction was always clear, whether you liked it or not. His only request was that we did not seek to publicise our work or communicate with external agencies without his approval. As a bonus, he approved Wi-Fi compatible Xboxes, knowing full well that it was a contentious decision for a governor to make. The potential ability to communicate remotely, however unlikely, has security implications. But as long as it was authorised, that wasn't our concern, and a win like this was vital to our image as a fledgling council.

Telfor always made sure he attended council meetings in person, as he knew we might have to raise an issue about a senior manager, an issue that could otherwise be brushed under the carpet if raised with the manager directly. True to his word, he once reprimanded one of his senior leadership team for giving Mark and me a hard time for nothing more than being members of the council.

For some staff, seeing prisoners on a 'council' was a challenge to their perceptions of how things ought to be and we sometimes received begrudging comments.

'No problem,' we'd say with a smile on our faces. 'We'll pass on your concerns to the governor.'

'Oh, no, no. I think the council's a wonderful idea,' the officer would respond.

But the council worked because it eased the burden on staff and gave prisoners a voice in the matters that affected them. Though there was one time when we did get a little bit carried away. We turned up to one meeting with a list of around 200 items.

In typical fashion, Telfor slumped back in his chair and said, 'So what are you lot going to do for the prison?'

We all looked at each other as if to say, 'Fair point.' As councillors, our role involved more than just representing the prisoners – we had a duty to represent the prison too and be responsible councillors, and that can often get lost in the race to accumulate kudos from your peers.

Being on the council gave us an insight into the challenges governors faced and how far public relations had seeped into the thinking of those in charge of our prisons, even when it came at the cost of initiatives that had a positive impact.

The prison's charity football tournament was an annual event at Gartree that had been going for decades, which benefited the community and raised money for charity. But some prison staff across the system had got themselves into the habit of selling one-sided appraisals of such events to tabloid newspapers. Sure enough, the tournament received negative press reports about murderers playing football and all future charity events were cancelled.

At the next meeting I raised this with Governor Telfor. I found his uncharacteristic apprehension confusing.

'Why don't you just contact the media and tell them the event raised money for charity?' I asked.

Telfor shook his head. 'Can't do it.'

'Why?' I continued. 'If people know the truth, then they'll be more accepting of these events.'

'Tell them how much we raised!' insisted another council member.

'It's called the *Daily Mail* test,' said Telfor. 'If the Prison Service thinks an idea might attract the disapproval of the *Daily Mail*, we don't do it.'

Now that Chris Grayling had settled into his new role, a Prison Service scheme called benchmarking was being rolled out. Its aim was to bring staff numbers in line with private-sector prisons, which employed fewer staff. Alongside this unexpected change, the core day was also being streamlined, which meant a little less time out of cell and fewer gym sessions for prisoners.

To adapt to this new regime, prisoners started training on the wing more frequently. On some days, nearly every landing had at least one group of prisoners doing pull-ups from a door frame or sprawled out doing push-ups. Boxing, Brazilian jiu-jitsu and wrestling were taking up my spare time. Along with Gaz and a group of friends, I committed endless hours to learning these arts and immersing myself in the technique. It no doubt seems like an unusual or undesirable hobby for people serving time for committing serious acts of violence but compared to the negativity that often occurred on a prison wing, it was considered OK by many staff and they mostly turned a blind eye. Governors, however, do not have the authority to approve martial arts in prisons, let alone allow them on prison landings.

Yet grappling was a positive experience for me. Understood properly, martial arts are as much about the mind as the body. Volatile people are certainly better off avoiding training in martial arts until they have at least developed the cognitive skills to control themselves, but the self-discipline and self-assurance gained from the practice of grappling cannot be understated. Anything that encourages self-reflection, problem-solving under stress and character building has the potential to assist with rehabilitation.

During the years I spent grappling, I developed the ability to visualise and problem-solve, two skills that would go on to make an invaluable contribution to my life. It also played a part in teaching me that it's not someone's physical abilities that make them dangerous, it's their state of mind.

On many occasions in prison, I witnessed physically weaker or mentally insecure men trying to prove themselves. Some people use violence and aggression because they have deep insecurities about themselves and are afraid of them being exposed. Although it doesn't seem like it, they judge carefully who to target, exploiting weaknesses as they arise. This helps them to maintain their façade, acting dangerous while secretly living in fear.

A typical example of this was one guy on the wing who was physically very slight and timid, but extremely gobby. He'd always get a gang of lads together before he acted and, on one occasion, he tried to rob an older guy on the wing who they thought was an easy target. Unfortunately for them, he turned on them with a pool cue – and they all ran off. But that didn't mean these people couldn't be dangerous and it was important to keep an eye on them and not show any weakness.

When I was doing jiu-jitsu training with people, I always tried to make sure we were polite and respectful to those around us, because one thing we didn't want to do was intimidate our fellow prisoners, to make them feel uncomfortable to the point that they might complain to the staff and hinder our training sessions – or worse, land us with a negative report.

Understanding the psychology of my peers was another motivation in my impulse to train, especially as the atmosphere at Gartree was beginning to change. Treating people with respect can go a long way, but only so far in some of today's prisons. Having physical presence acts as another layer of protection. It keeps the wolves guessing and while they are guessing, they are not attacking. All that's often needed is the impression of strength. When the wolves hunt the elks, they always go for the one that looks the weakest.

★

Early on in my time at Gartree, when I threw myself into education, I met Stephen, one of the mentors in the IT class I took. Stephen told me that he ran a chess club in the prison and, given that I'd been playing chess in Frankland, I thought it was a good opportunity to 'kill some bird' and to improve my game.

It turned out that Stephen was obsessed with chess. A bit older than me, his cell was piled high with chess books and he was a very good player. He became the perfect person to learn from and develop – if you want to get better, you have to play the best. On the weekends in particular, a group of us would get together on the corridor with some chess boards and play. At the weekend, the wing could get quite hectic: people are getting drunk and getting up to all sorts, and I preferred to escape and do something productive. Not that chess is all *that* productive, of course, but it does engage your brain and it kills time.

I came to see the parallels between the game and my sentence. There are different ways you can play the game of chess, just as there are different ways to serve your time. You can play the long game but you've got to be tactical and strategic about how you go about meeting your objectives – just like my sentence. My ultimate objective, of course, was getting out, but I had to be strategic and tactical in how I did that. So I felt chess strengthened those elements of my mindset. And some chess games are like a war of attrition, just as a sentence in many ways is too. Patience and self-control are virtues that come in handy for both. During my time at Gartree, chess became very important to me. I played and played and played, and I can see now that it also offered an escape route for my mind. I improved dramatically, even topping the league eventually, though, for me, in the words of Jez, it was always more about the journey than the destination.

As I moved on through my sentence, I would have other objectives to meet: different prisons would present different things as I moved a little closer to getting out, and chess would become less important to me. But right now, it offered my mind some much-needed freedom within the confines of the prison system. Yet playing chess and training jiu-jitsu weren't the only things I would use to pass my time. Through a fortuitous encounter, I would discover yet another great way to creatively engage my brain.

I was walking up the staircase one day when a prisoner who had not long arrived, called Stewey, wandered past with a broken guitar in his hand. The strings were snapped and hanging off, some of the tuning pegs had come loose and it looked like it had been left under someone's bed for several years. It was one of those classical-style guitars, mainly used for fingerpicking.

'What are you doing with that, mate?' I asked.

'Someone's just given it to me, but I'm throwing it in the bin. It's knackered,' Stewey responded while looking pitifully at what was basically a tattered piece of wood in his hand.

'Gis it here,' I said. 'I'll have a go at fixing it.'

I couldn't play the guitar but I'd always been pretty good with my hands, so I took it back to my cell. Over the next few weeks, I set about stripping it down, sanding and applying a fresh layer of varnish, fixing the tuning pegs and buying new strings. To add a finishing touch, I paid a prison tattooist to draw a floral pattern onto the body of the guitar before giving it one last touch of varnish.

When I went to return it to Stewey, he was so impressed he asked me to keep it and offered to teach me how to play the guitar. It turned out that Stewey had been playing the Blues for over thirty years and could play lead guitar with his eyes shut. So I ended up spending many hours practising with Stewey following our moment on the stairs. I never really did get any good at playing, but I had stumbled across another pastime to drain away the hours of my sentence, and ended up developing a greater appreciation for the skill of guitarists and the amazing, captivating sound of the guitar.

CHAPTER 15

A Perfect Storm

Time passes in prison much faster than it does in society. The years were passing like the seasons – and it was beginning to make me feel uneasy. With each day being so similar, there is less information for the memory to use to differentiate one day from the next, so it smooths the passage of time. Before I knew it, four years at Gartree had slipped by and I was now halfway through my sentence.

Things had been changing at Gartree during that time. The increases in longer sentences had been creating pressure across the cat A system and that pressure could only go in one direction – down, towards the category B establishments. Rather than receive prisoners following a lengthy stint in the high-security estate, which can have a settling effect, Gartree had been accepting men almost immediately after sentence, or after they had served only a year or so in category A prisons. As a result, some of the conflicts that were still being played out across cat As and their inevitable consequences began to trickle through.

Over the course of just four years, Gartree's laid-back atmosphere became a distant memory, thanks largely to the gang-related issues ingrained in cat As that were now filtering at pace into the category B system. That uneasy feeling that loomed in the atmosphere at Frankland was back, complete with the constant possibility of violence and the sale of drugs – though this time it was a new drug that was in demand.

Spice arrived at Gartree in 2013. A highly addictive, low-cost, synthetic drug, it was a new socially destructive problem to manage. Spice could be sprayed onto an A4 sheet of paper and sent through the post disguised as a letter, making it ideal for smuggling. If a tiny piece of paper smaller than the size of a fingernail could fetch around £10, it's not hard to imagine how an A4 book could bring in thousands. Not only is spice highly addictive, it contains unknown properties that are extremely harmful to the nervous system. Fits, mental breakdowns, psychosis, self-harm and an increase in mental health issues are just some of the common side effects. Witnessing one of my neighbours convulsing on the floor or doubling over after having a spice attack soon became a familiar sighting on C Wing. Some lads would never be the same again after taking it.

I first heard about spice when one guy returned to Gartree having left about a year earlier. When I saw him he very quickly told me, 'I've been taking this thing called Spice – it's fucking brilliant.' He'd just been brought back to prison, having had the opportunity to be released, and yet all he could talk about was this drug and how good it was. Spice flooded the system shortly afterwards.

According to legend in other prisons, one guy was said to have cut off his own penis and another removed his own eye because, it was purported, he could not remove an image of the devil from his retina. Even though these horror tales were well known, such was the addictive lure of spice that it became the drug of choice even for seasoned addicts who'd taken crack and heroin for most their lives. Rather than being put off by its potency, prisoners were attracted to it because it was viewed as getting more for less.

Aiyden Johnson, a mixed-race lad who'd converted to Islam while at HMP Whitemore, was a smart dresser, approachable and full of energy. He told me that his fancy wardrobe was paid for by his partner. Despite Aiyden's impressive façade, however, he would take any mind-altering substance he could get his hands on. Inevitably, Aiyden would make the transition to spice, now the most popular drug on the market.

Living with people like Aiyden enabled me to truly understand the damage that drugs cause, not only to the lives of the user but to their loved ones too.

'Let her go, Aiyden,' folk would say to him.

'I've told her to go, but she won't listen,' he would reply unconvincingly.

To maintain his habit, the woman who became his wife ended up selling her house and she once found herself barred from the prison after getting caught bringing in contraband during a visit.

Inside Time is the national newspaper for prisoners, a monthly printed edition that provides all sorts of useful information about the world we inhabit. Prisoners can also write in about their gripes, ask questions or offer each other advice. It was while reading *Inside Time* one day that I came across an article from a Gartree prisoner written under a pseudonym. The author had encouraged prisoners at other prisons to lobby their respective governors to approve Xbox 360s with Wi-Fi, in keeping with the recent policy change at Gartree.

I bumped into Mark later that afternoon.

'Have you seen that article in *Inside Time*?' I asked. 'Which idiot's done that?'

'Oh,' he responded casually, 'that was me.'

'What?'

Mark was just being Mark, trying to make sure as many prisoners could benefit as possible. But it was never going to go down well with Telfor.

At our next council meeting, Telfor walked into the room fuming and slammed himself down into his chair. 'What did I say to you lot about communicating with outside agencies?'

'You told us not to do it, Governor,' we responded sheepishly.

Mark remained quiet, hoping to slip under his radar.

Then Telfor suddenly turned. 'And you!' he shouted at Mark, pointing his finger at him. 'You're lucky I don't have you shipped out to Long Lartin!'

Telfor was never really going to do that but he did reverse his decision on the Xboxes, meaning all those prisoners who had spent hundreds of pounds purchasing one were suddenly out of pocket as they were gradually confiscated. And poor Mark had a lot of pleading to do after some very serious threats to his safety were made by other prisoners.

Aside from the risk of pissing off your fellow prisoners for failing to achieve the things they wanted, being on the Prisoner Council had many privileges, like inter-wing travel, meetings during lockdown and being the first to hear from the governor about changes to local and national policy. The council was even updated about the latest scientific knowledge on the composition of spice. But if a directive came from Prison Service headquarters, it was generally unwelcome news.

In November 2013, Chris Grayling authorised the most draconian Prison Service Instruction (PSI) to have ever been issued. PSI 30/2013 altered the IEP (Incentives and Earned Privileges) scheme, the rules that govern what prisoners can and cannot have, making it far harder for us to receive family visits or money from loved ones. Among many other unnecessary measures, Grayling banned educational books and guitar strings, and prevented prisoners from having photos during visits with their families and friends.

With austerity measures now taking effect in all areas of justice, the benchmarking programme, in which public-service prisons were required to bring their costs in line with private-sector prisons, could not have come at a worse time. Since operational employees are the largest expenditure, this area was hit the hardest, resulting in a 30 per cent reduction in frontline staff over a three-year period from 2014. Benchmarking did include replacing some frontline staff with new recruits on cut-rate contracts, but not only did the recruitment drive fail to materialise, those who were employed had fewer experienced officers to show them the ropes. Both the quantity and quality of staff were impacted.

As for the staff that did remain, due to their increased workloads and the heightened risk to their safety, they felt unappreciated and let down by their bosses in London. As a result, staff morale plummeted, which also had a deteriorating effect on their ability to both interact with prisoners and manage any escalating situations. The stability of a regime is highly reliant on constructive relationships between staff and prisoners, but these new policies served only to undermine this.

My feeling was that all of this created a perfect storm in which the wings became more violent and the staff's ability to police it was severely compromised. It seemed to me at times that staff morale was so bad that they would almost step back and allow things to happen rather than put themselves on the line to stamp out problems. And who could blame them? The wings had become violent places and there was a very real risk they might come to harm in doing their jobs.

These changes presented serious challenges to those whose aim in prison was rehabilitation and progression through the system. It's hard to concentrate on the vital work required to do this, whether through violence reduction courses or through individual education endeavours, when tensions are high on the wing, anxiety rises and the prospect of violence or disturbance increases dramatically.

One reason why private prisons are said to run so effectively with fewer staff is because they use technology to deliver vital services and provide extra privileges to ensure prisoner compliance. For example, they have access to in-cell telephones and a wider range of food items that can be ordered from an in-cell interface. And prisoners receive higher pay for work at private prisons. With most public-sector prisons lacking the technology to assist with managing prisoners' daily needs, it meant that the reduction in staff numbers alongside the tightening up of the privileges scheme left the prison system with a diminished control mechanism.

When Chris Grayling took office and set out on an ideological warpath, he clearly didn't foresee the damage he was about to cause to the prison system. Though it's not surprising he was going to make a hash of things. He was the first Justice Secretary without a legal background to hold that position in modern times, and prior to taking his post, he'd apparently never entered a prison in his life.

At a time when prisons were grossly overcrowded, scattered with IPP prisoners, polluted with spice, and violent gangs with an ideological twist prowled the landings, aggressive staff cuts were the straw that finally broke the camel's back. Almost overnight, thousands of experienced staff had disappeared and the beast that is our prison system was brought crashing to its knees.

And if things weren't bad enough, Governor Telfor was moving on to another establishment, a departure that would leave the prison without a full-time governor for the next few years.

With the abrupt depletion of frontline staff came a perceptible absence of authority on the landings. And this was no more satisfying to anyone than the gangs and violent prisoners who were now inhabiting C Wing, where I had resided for the previous five years. A power shift had effectively taken place. But unlike at Frankland, it was not from prisoners to prisoners; it was from state to prisoners.

There are six main houseblocks at Gartree, each holding between 100 and 120 prisoners. C Wing sat among a group of houseblocks that were closed plan, four floors high with a tiny office on the ground floor. The layout meant that violence could be committed out of sight and earshot of staff. So not only were they lacking the ability to intervene, they were often unaware when trouble was even occurring. Yet another factor that left prisoners vulnerable to the new arrivals at Gartree.

Two groups of prisoners had now begun to establish themselves on C Wing. One was made up mostly of British black and mixed-race men whose priorities leaned more towards establishing authority and generating returns from the sale of drugs. The other was of British Pakistani origin, with more religion-based interests. Both were effectively operating as gangs, since they were well organised, lived off the proceeds of drug sales and used coordinated group violence to achieve their aims. Although the core of each group was not fond of the other, they had affiliates that cross-associated and their mutual reliance on the Islamic faith gave them an excuse to avoid conflict with each other.

What had originally been used by religious extremists to strengthen their hand was now being more deliberately exploited by individuals with widening agendas, the most obvious being the sale of drugs. Violent prisoners who adhered more strictly to their religion were still filtering through but the new arrivals were far more criminally orientated than religious. And when considering the effectiveness of the network to guarantee protection to its members, converting to Islam was seen as a small concession to make. Whether any of these individuals genuinely believed in its divine authority almost became superfluous; maintaining the impression was what counted.

When the British Army soldier Lee Rigby was murdered in London on 22 May 2013 by terrorists Michael Adebolajo and Michael Adebowale, some prisoners could be heard shouting 'Allahu Akbar' from their windows. Like the howls of wolves, euphoric window-warrior moments would often follow news reports of a terrorist attack. And these guys were not hardened terrorists like those held in category As: they were British-born, British-educated citizens.

The multi-faith centre had always become a mosque on Fridays but this was taken over so that it was no longer just a place of worship but a networking space where illicit activities could be carried out with limited interference from prison security. It seemed a far cry from the tea and biscuits I used to enjoy in the chapel at HMP Hull. By professing to represent the Muslim faith, the men who were engaging in violence and criminal activities were giving the impression that what was on display was Islam, or at least was justified by it. To the practising Muslim prisoners for whom their religion was a genuine and important aspect of their life, the infiltration of the mosque for illicit purposes was highly insulting. But what could they do about it? No one wanted to take on the gangs.

I would occasionally train with a practising Muslim called Bilal, whose faith was central to his existence. He was one of the most peaceful guys I'd ever met. It was Bilal who once told me that jihad was a central part of Islam and that one part involved an internal struggle called 'greater jihad', which meant focusing on yourself internally. Anyone who tries to better themselves internally is bound to be more at peace and accepting of others. Bilal seemed to embody this, in contrast to the men who appeared more concerned with status, material gain and power.

'Guess what I've just seen,' said a prisoner excitedly, running from door to door to spread the news. 'Them two queers shagging each other.'

'Fuck off, you lying cunt,' said another prisoner flippantly.

'I'm telling ya. I fucking heard 'em.'

The two men in question were openly gay, so most prisoners just rolled their eyes, thinking no more of it. But it was not taken so lightly by one of the gangs, who paid someone to enter their cell in a balaclava to carry out a punishment beating.

From what I'd seen during my time inside, homophobia had largely faded as an issue in prisons. Yes, there would always be people happy to snigger or deliver a derogatory comment, but by and large it wasn't really seen as a big deal. But after one of these chaps had his nose broken during his beating, it became clear that same-sex acts were now unofficially outlawed.

But while one cultural idea seemed to be regressing, another was progressing. What had originally seemed a racial division was beginning to change shape into something more complicated, along quasi-religious lines. The number of prisoners of different racial backgrounds converting to Islam had significantly increased over the years, and this was particularly true of white inmates.

Such was the ease with which some of the white converts could be influenced, they were often employed to inflict violence on prisoners from their own race, which allowed the gangs another avenue of attack and avoided the perception of racism. The issue of race had seemingly disappeared as a dividing line, while religion had been well and truly promoted.

Sometimes, however, exceptions have to be made. Aiyden Johnson might have been a practising Muslim, but that didn't stop him from getting a kicking from one of the gangs for not paying his debts. It was reasoned that because Aiyden was taking drugs, he was not a proper Muslim, which neatly ignored the contradiction that his attackers were the ones who had sold the drugs to him in the first place.

CHAPTER 16

The Violence Reduction Programme

Finally, an opportunity had come up for me to complete the violence reduction programme, an eight-month course designed to reduce the likelihood of violence and aggression in offenders by identifying risks and providing tools for managing them. The VRP attempts this complicated task from a social and psychological perspective.

Prior to the start of the course, the VRP facilitators identified several risk factors that were considered to increase my chances of reoffending. The most significant of these were my attitude towards violence, peer pressure and substance misuse. Cognitive distortions, emotional control and problem-solving were other features that were raised. A five-stage model called 'the Stages of Change' was then used to determine a starting point for the treatment I required for each of the identified risks. The first was 'pre-contemplation', which means an individual has no awareness of their problem (such as issues with alcohol). The second was 'contemplation', which means they are aware of the issue causing them difficulties and want to do something about it; followed by 'preparation', planning change; 'action', putting it into practice; and 'maintenance'.

So, for example, where substance misuse was concerned, I was in the action stage. In fact, most of my risk factors were in the later phases set out by the Stages of Change and this almost prevented me from being accepted for the course. The reason they allowed me to do it was because I had waited almost eight years for the opportunity.

Alongside ten other men with varying histories of violence and antisocial behaviour, I settled in to complete the course. Yet it didn't take long for our group to dwindle in size. Within the first month, two were shipped out after being involved in a mini riot on D Wing; another went berserk on C Wing after smoking too much Spice; another had a fight on his wing and, in the final week of the course, one of them suddenly became aggressive towards a psychologist quietly watching the session.

'What you looking at?' he snapped.

'I . . . I'm not looking at you,' stuttered the shocked psychologist. 'I'm just craning my neck so I can hear you speak.'

'You keep looking at me,' he continued, on camera and in front of six other psychologists. 'You're making me paranoid. I don't like it when people look at me.'

Out of all the offending behaviour courses I enrolled on during my sentence, I found the VRP the most benefi-cial. It helped me to better understand the social origin of my thinking and behaviour and how my psychological make-up led me to respond in the way that I did on the night of my offence. One of my tasks was to write a short autobiography on my upbringing and it was during that process that I really began to appreciate the foundations of my violence.

Being hit for misbehaving was customary when I was young, a practice that was ramped up considerably with the arrival of my stepfather when I was nine years old, and continued until I reached the age of fifteen. It's also possible that I was suffering with an attention deficit disorder, but identifying and treating the condition only became widespread in more recent times, so I will never truly know about this. What I do know is that even with my best efforts I was unable to concentrate in class. As a result, I was labelled a 'naughty' child and treated as such.

Since my stepfather's child-management skills consisted of using violence and aggression, this had two effects on me: physically, I became very good at absorbing strikes to the body, and mentally, I subconsciously formed a belief that it was acceptable to use violence and aggression to resolve issues.

It was during the VRP that I learned about the significance of beliefs in the decision-making process. Before they are formed, parts of the brain begin their existence like blank pieces of software that load up with information through our senses. This process forms our beliefs, which are central to how we make sense of the world. They shape our values, inform our reasoning, give us a sense of identity and influence how we respond to those around us. It is during our early years that most of our fundamental beliefs are formed. Six years is a long time to be beaten by an adult.

Each slap, kick and punch helped write the instructions that would determine how I dealt with certain types of problems in my life. And as I was often exposed to violence outside the home, there was very little to offset these encounters. On it went; underachieving at school meant I gravitated towards children with similar behaviour to mine. Unhealthy attachments formed and, on a trajectory followed by many before me, I absorbed the ill-fated wisdom of other street kids on the estates of East Hull, which included criminal values and codes that bonded me to my immediate peer group and eventually detached me, to some degree, from my family and community. All this was reinforced through exciting encounters typical of British working-class culture, like kicking the shit out of other lads while drunk and evading the police afterwards.

With low self-esteem and surrounded by males jostling for status, I built up a façade to hide my insecurities. We all have one – how we prefer the world to see us – but it's just that some have a more carefully constructed one than others. And mine remained, along with my beliefs and criminal values about life, largely unchecked, until the age of twenty-eight, when I committed the offence for which I was serving.

None of this means I was walking around frothing at the mouth and looking for fights, of course. I was easy-going and disciplined enough to work for a living. I simply had a deep-rooted piece of coding which activated in certain scenarios that professionals refer to as 'high-risk situations'. From a social and psychological perspective, it explained a lot.

On the night Jayne was attacked, my learned reaction was to resolve the issue with violence. My susceptibility to peer pressure part-influenced me to carry out what I assumed my immediate peer group expected of me. My emotions clouded my judgement and my cognitive distortions meant I was also concerned about looking weak if I didn't respond with violence. As I lacked critical self-awareness and a decent set of problem-solving skills, all of the above went unchecked. Furthermore, on the evening that I stumbled across my victim, I was drunk and if anything can exacerbate an existing bundle of cognitive deficiencies stacked on top of a violent disposition, it's alcohol.

Of course, I'm also programmed as nature intended: to feel intense protective urges and perhaps vengeful impulses when someone invades my home and harms my kin. I was not born to resolve issues through violence. But so entrenched was my belief that it was acceptable to use violence and aggression to resolve certain issues, I was essentially walking the streets without a clue that I possessed a very serious capacity to harm others. This insight explained why my predicament following my arrest felt so profoundly at odds with what I really wanted in life. That is the power of beliefs.

While completing courses like the VRP, I discovered a great deal about myself. I learned that certain experiences and ideas, whether they are instilled through a kick, through an adventure or whispered by an associate, can capture the mind and ultimately lead its owner to destruction. But when I looked outside my own story, I was left with further questions. Why did my brother, who had been raised in the same household, not hold the same beliefs as me about violence? And if the VRP was such a highly rated course, why were so many participants impervious to its treatment methods? I came to learn too that there may well be other answers that explain why some people might be more susceptible than others to harmful social influences or can go through life without genuinely being able to control their behaviour. Rather than nurture being in the dock, this time it was nature.

Not long after I'd completed the VRP I came across a book called *The Anatomy of Violence* by Dr Adrian Raine, a neuroscientist whose research shows how biological factors – such as the structure of the brain, resting heart rate, genetics, head injury and even poor nutrition – can predispose a person to violent and risk-taking behaviour in adulthood. These factors, he points out, are typically present in the profiles of serial killers and psychopaths. It was what he wrote about two parts of the brain – the amygdala and the striatum – that I found most useful for the points I would like to make.

The smaller the amygdala – the part of the brain responsible for emotional responses, among other things – the more likely it is that someone will lack fear and confront danger. This effect on human performance is more commonly understood through the phrase, 'fight or flight'. Whereas the striatum, the part of the brain that is stimulated when reward is anticipated, plays an important role in driving behaviours like addiction. The larger the striatum, the more someone may disregard the negative consequences of risk-taking behaviour as the internal reward system is stimulated.

A small amygdala or an enlarged striatum do not in themselves predestine violence or recklessness in adulthood, but these variations do increase the chances of them emerging if the owner is exposed to violence or raised in a deprived social setting during childhood.

Although I have no idea whether I have any of these variations, they do explain how two children raised under the same conditions could turn out quite differently. And conceivably, they might also explain how my fellow participant on the VRP could become aggressive towards a psychologist in the final minutes of an eight-month programme designed to reduce violence and aggression. As helpful as the VRP was in identifying the social and psychological factors that lead some individuals to violence and anti-social behaviours, something was clearly missing.

Violence is not inevitable in adulthood, there is evidence to show that. But if hidden factors like those described by Dr Adrian Raine are present while things like socially unacceptable behaviours or inferior problem-solving skills are instilled within us, then it is reasonable to assume that our behaviours may manifest in raw and unforgiving ways.

And yet, if some of the forces I know affected me are so dominant, how was I able to resist using violence and aggression from so early in my sentence? After I'd completed the VRP, I asked a psychologist for her professional opinion as to why I had suddenly felt less comfortable about violence and aggression, why I had been able to turn my back on them. She explained that my experience was possibly similar to someone who had lived through a traumatic event like a car crash. Following a near death experience, some people suddenly begin to appreciate their life more, spending time with family, eating better and worrying less about trivialities. In short, the impact of the experience develops a new belief that alters their outlook on life. Fundamentally, my catalyst for change was the shattering of the ideas by which I'd been living. That experience opened a crack through which I could peer into the depths of my mind. And once that had happened, I could not unsee what I had seen. Like a Damascene conversion, it changed me forever.

Yet it did not guarantee absolute change. When your behaviours have been ingrained since childhood, it still takes commitment and determination to fashion your insights into something positive. And it's another thing to do this in the presence of those who will consider it a rejection of their values (which it is) or a form of weakness (which it isn't). Prison culture is made up of an us-and-them mentality that is enforced by men with powerful egos and their followers who place pressure on their peers to adhere to a prisoner/criminal code. Going against the grain can leave you ostracised or, worse, exposed to violence. It's no joke, especially in the higher categories of the prison system.

But I had no choice except to swallow my history of poor choices and begin the journey of peeling back the layers of my façade so I could confront my demons. Without that, I would not have been able to draw forth the real person who lived inside me, the individual who was not born to be violent for the sake of it. Needless to say, this continued to be balanced against the reality of prison life. Like everyone else, my instinct to survive was firing away, accelerating my decision making as I navigated the evolving threats on the prison landings.

Although I was now making a conscious effort to reject my old behaviour, my upbringing in Hull had at least given me an intuitive understanding of how to survive among those who used violence and manipulation as a way of life. Without that, I might not have had the ability to avoid the problems that were continuing to develop on C Wing.

CHAPTER 17

The End of Tolerance

It was never an easy task trying to square with the prison population the policies that were passed down to the Prisoner Council from above. Our power was limited in what we could actually achieve and in many ways we were just the messenger. But in a climate where people were prone to getting angry and confrontational, the phrase 'don't shoot the messenger' wasn't of much use. We would often be asked by other prisoners to make unreasonable requests from the governor, such as allowing prisoners to purchase their own TVs or Sky boxes, and this could cause frustration whenever we refused. At times, it felt like a balancing act to deliver the often disappointing information, represent the prisoners and, crucially, keep both the prisoners and staff happy with what we were trying to do. But the knowledge and experience we gained was priceless.

The council was made up of a group of seven councillors, including a vice-chair and a chair. Each member of the council was responsible for a certain area – say, visits or the canteen – which meant if a prisoner had an issue about visits, they could come and see you and then you would take it up with a senior manager. The council decided among ourselves who got which area – and those areas that were deemed to have the most kudos would often be allocated after a lengthy debate. Though it could be a case of being careful what you wished for: in each of the areas the work was largely the same, but for those carrying more kudos it meant that the person responsible would often get more attention from the prison population – which is great when things go well but not so good when they don't.

In 2015, I ran for a second term and was re-elected by 150 of my peers. After taking the chair for a brief while, I stepped aside to accept the position of vice-chair. This time, we had five Muslim councillors on board, reflecting both the change in Gartree's population and the Council's growing popularity as a resource for voicing our concerns. But not all prisoners were happy with the Prisoner Council.

One day, a prisoner approached me and asked if he could speak to me one on one. Once the room had emptied following a council meeting, I called him over.

'Come in, mate,' I said. 'Take a seat.'

'Take a seat!' he snapped. 'Take a fucking seat!' He bowled towards me, pointing his finger. 'I'll cut your fucking throat. Who the fuck do you think you are? Take a fucking seat . . .' He stopped within reaching distance. 'You lot on the council think you're summat fucking special.'

Experience had taught me that people in prison who are serious about hurting you don't usually tell you what they are going to do beforehand. Nor was he carrying anything in his hand. That said, his emotions had got the better of him, so, although I remained calm, I was primed.

'You lot walk around like you fucking own the place,' he continued.

'I apologise if I've upset you. That wasn't my intention,' I said calmly.

Now he was staring at me with a self-assured smirk but at least he wasn't physically attacking me.

In times gone by, I would almost certainly have responded aggressively, but to do so now would have undone years of resistance and commitment. Random and unprovoked acts of aggression are common in prisons and if you reacted aggressively to every single one of them, you'd be fighting every day. In the end, my non-confrontational manner worked because he eventually calmed down and we ended up discussing what he wanted to talk about in the first place.

By his own admission, the way we carried ourselves as council members had challenged his views about how prisoners ought to express themselves. But this chap was not only a good example of someone who had limited insights into his own thinking and behaviour – despite having recently completed the VRP – he also put himself at risk.

In a flash of anger, he had assessed my attributes based solely on my role as a council member and in doing so he had overlooked the fact that I was at the peak of my physical and mental fitness. Whatever it was that stimulated his initial assessment of me, his emotions had very quickly taken over. We all have the capacity to prejudge but anger not only distorts our judgement, it obscures danger. Anger communicated aggressively only increases the chances of arousing anger and therefore the same blindness in your opponent. If that happens, not only have you lost control of yourself but of your opponent too. Then anything is possible.

As the conditions began to deteriorate at Gartree, the multi-faith centre became one of the few places where I could avoid having to watch people getting their heads kicked in. Along with some friends, Bible studies and the gospel choir became regular features in my diary. I'd come to realise that the best way to test your beliefs and values is to open yourself up to the stuff that contradicts it, so I stopped debating and started listening more. Though it's fair to say that my decision to tone things down a bit was somewhat enforced: I felt welcome at the church and didn't want to come across as ungrateful, while back on C Wing it had become too risky to express any opinions about the fundamental nature of the universe. The mix of prisoners beginning to arrive had far more uncompromising views on faith and doctrine. The last thing I wanted was for anyone to take offence at my cold logic and reason.

Two of these new arrivals were Omar Shaffi and Nadeem Mohammod, who had arrived at Gartree in 2014/15. Omar, who always wore a prayer gown and a beard down to his chest, was formerly known as Richard Pratt, a white British lad who began his sentence attacking Muslim prisoners in Frankland. Omar was easy to get on with but he had a rather morbid obsession with violence.

'I'd do anything for my brothers,' he once told me.

After serving up (stabbing and slashing) another prisoner at HMP Swaleside with a group of like-minded prisoners, he was awaiting another sentence for GBH. According to Omar, the crime was far worse than the charge suggested. Some prisoners converted out of fear of the gangs and extremists but Omar was not one of them. He was committed.

And so was his friend Nadeem, who had just begun a 24-year sentence for murder. Formally known as Robby Clarke, Nadeem was another white British convert who was equally keen about Islam being enforced through violence and intimidation. He refused to speak to white people unless they were Muslim and his ambition was to join his brothers in cat As, a wish he was later granted after violently attacking a prison officer.

The arrival of individuals like this added another unsettling edge to Gartree's environment, which began to suck in some of the most vulnerable. And even those who seemed not so vulnerable.

'They've got to him,' I heard an officer remark.

Wang Lei, a Chinese national who was serving 28 years for murder, was an intelligent man. He'd grasped the English language so quickly that within just a couple of years we were discussing international politics and his life back home in China. We also practised the guitar together, a pastime that was abruptly terminated following his conversion. The prison Imam informed 'Shakar', as he was now known, that if he wanted to be a Muslim, he could no longer practise the guitar or listen to Western music.

Although more extreme in their own right, the new arrivals were affiliated to the Pakistani group. And not too long after they had settled, they began praying on the landings. There's nothing wrong with praying, of course; it is a right. It's just not pleasant having a group of men who ten minutes earlier were booting someone up and down the landing praying on your doorstep.

After prison managers approved praying in Gartree's education block during lessons, staff were left powerless to intervene in what were essentially symbolic displays of the group's growing authority. When you have violent individuals with unresolved psychological issues carrying out this practice in full view, you'd expect more caution. It was an attempt by the authorities to appease growing demands from a changing demographic, but by neglecting to use their common sense, prison managers were further assisting the transition of influence.

With the alarm bells ringing, the incident that had taken place was possibly encouraged by this approach to managing inmates. During a routine fabric check – which used to be called bolts and bars, in which the cells would be routinely checked to make sure everything was secure and in order – a rookie officer stumbled across a mobile phone in someone's cell. As he was walking away from the landing to report his find, he was grabbed by a group of prisoners and had the phone forcefully taken from him. By the time the officer was able to break free and raise the alarm, the phone had been whisked away. It was unheard of for a group of lifers to physically restrain an officer, as the consequences of engaging in concerted action against a prison's security in this manner can be severe, both in the short and long-term. In this instance, however, the risk may have been worth it. Not long after, one of their group confided in an associate of mine that the phone had been used to contact a member of Isis in the Middle East. Fortunately for them, the rookie officer was unable to identify which prisoners had grabbed him and the phone was never found.

Whether or not the contact with Isis was genuine, it certainly fit with what was happening on C Wing, where some prisoners were openly expressing their support for Isis and displaying the Isis flag in their cells. When approached by an officer about this decorative display of allegiance, the owner of one of the flags simply replied, 'The flag is symbolic to all Muslims.'

Indeed, the flag used by Isis does have an important meaning in Islam but this was 2015, a time when sectarian conflicts in Iraq and Syria were in full swing; Isis had established a self-declared caliphate and jihadists were running riot across parts of the Middle East and North Africa. Across Europe too, a number of devastating terrorist attacks had taken place, like that at the office of French satirical newspaper *Charlie Hebdo* on 7 January 2015.

These events, plastered across the world's news channels, were not only acting as sources of inspiration to Islamists, they were influencing the minds of some of our prisoners. And the availability of smartphones in prisons meant that extremists and the impressionable could watch less sanitised versions of those same events – or possibly even communicate with those involved.

To people across the world, including the many Muslims who were the biggest victims of terrorism and jihadists, there was nothing more disturbing than watching the images of Isis militias riding on the back of stolen tanks as they rolled into defenceless communities to slaughter the innocent. To those who were psychologically predisposed to violence and extremism, including certain prisoners on C Wing, these images not only validated their ideas about life, it gave them an uplifting sense of self-worth. For the prisoners who just wanted to get on with their sentences, the timing could not have been worse.

Following 2005, the rise of religious extremism in prisons was always going to pose a challenge to prison authorities; there were just too many independent factors involved for it not to become a problem in one form or another. But the conditions that enabled it to erupt into something more forceful were made far more favourable by the reduction in staff. Unfortunately, the Justice Secretary, Chris Grayling, would not be around to witness the most damaging effects of his legacy, as he vacated his role in May 2015.

One day in March 2016, I was leaning against the top-floor balcony of C Wing when five lads came marching up the stairway. One of them, Shakar (formerly known as Wang Lei), remained next to me while the other four headed straight towards the cell of Tim Carter, a young man who'd not long arrived from HMP Full Sutton, where he'd converted to Islam. The chap standing next to me kept an eye out while the others entered Tim's cell and gave him a sustained beating. After they'd left, Omar and Nadeem, not quite satisfied, went back for another go. Tim's crime? He'd allegedly thrown a Quran in a bin.

Given Tim's timid nature, their allegation was dubious. But what was most unusual about this incident was that out of the five lads who'd attacked him, only one, Imran Rehman, was born into the Muslim faith. The other four, Omar, Nadeem, Shakar and Aslam (a Welsh lad who would die later that year after consuming drugs), had converted to Islam while in prison.

After Tim was discovered by staff, he was locked behind his door. Though it didn't take long for him to be coerced back into the fold of Nadeem and Aslam, who advised him that if he kept his mouth shut, it would prove he was a 'good Muslim'.

What was also intriguing about the assault on Tim was its apparent sense of normality. As Wang Lei stood next to me on the stairway and I watched him out of the corner of my eye, he seemed completely oblivious to his behaviour. Before his recent conversion, Lei, as far as prisoners go, was peaceful and open-minded. From personal experience, I was aware of how beliefs could limit someone's self-awareness, but Lei's indoctrination into the faith-based brotherhood network not only happened at great speed, it happened while he was a mature adult with his ability to rationalise seemingly intact.

As much as I'd gone off violence, watching people getting bullied and beaten is not an easy thing to do. My perception of violence may have changed but it's never far away from your thoughts when it surrounds you. I always knew that I could be next, so there is an instinctive need to self-preserve. It was only because I was committed so firmly to my promise of non-violence that I resisted anything pre-emptive or retributive. Though there was one time when I nearly found myself in the firing line after I'd stepped in for a mate, a scouse lad called Micky.

One morning, Micky walked past Nadeem, who was wearing a prayer gown, and said to him, 'Fuck me, la, thought you was gonna blow me up then!'

Nadeem instantly squared up to Micky.

By chance, a few of us were nearby, so we stepped in to prevent a tear-up. But Micky was now on the hit list.

Wanting to prevent a potential bloodbath, later that afternoon I went to Omar's cell. As I entered, Omar, Nadeem and three others were still seething over Micky's comment and raring to go. I shut the door behind me.

'You know what he's like,' I said, trying to make light of it. 'He didn't mean anything by it.'

The thing is, he didn't, but fragile minds don't like humour. These guys seriously wanted to hurt him. Then the room suddenly fell silent, as if there was a collective shift of thought. The pack had spotted a vulnerability – I was isolated and they all looked at me as if to say, 'Who the fuck do you think you are?'

I pretended not to be alert to the sinister thoughts that had entered their minds. If I'd shown fear or acknowledged their status, that could have made the difference. If Omar and his brothers had attacked me with their knives, I would have stood no chance. Omar knew this; I saw it in his eyes.

Fortunately, after a few tense moments, one of their group calmed his brothers with his own light-hearted intervention and I managed to leave unscathed.

Micky's card, however, remained marked.

One day, I returned to the wing to find that Gaz had been stabbed in the back multiple times by his co-defendant, one of the gang leaders on C Wing who had converted to Islam in prison. The fallout was related to their joint conviction. Gaz was popular on the wing and a stand-off ensued between a large group of black lads and a large group of white lads.

With staff aware of the situation but lacking the means to do anything pre-emptive, they were left with no choice but to plead anxiously with passing members of each group: 'Think about the consequences, lads. It's not worth it!'

Many of those present were averaging sentences of between 25 and 35 years. With little to lose, it would have been a bloodbath had it kicked off. Fortunately, the Pakistani firm had opted to remain neutral, a decision which created less certainty that Gaz's co-defendant and his group could come away unscathed. The next day, however, Gaz was voluntarily removed from the prison and the matter was resolved. As for his co-defendant, not even a slap on the wrist from Gartree's authorities.

Gaz and I had arrived at the prison at the same time and had that link from day one; we'd become good training partners in the gym and bonded over rugby. In truth, I didn't get too close to many people in prison, focused as I was on working my way through it and changing my outlook on life. I tended to have people I'd play chess with, people I'd train with, but still, I considered Gaz to be a friend and was sorry to see him go.

That's what it's like for lifers. You get to know each other quite well due to the crazy lengths of time you're forced to spend together. But with today's life sentences increasingly spanning from two to four decades, if a sideways transfer takes place, which could be to any prison in the country, you sort of know you're never going to see them again.

CHAPTER 18

Faith in What, Exactly?

There had been a growing number of press reports about extremism in British prisons and on 5 April 2016, Gartree finally took its turn in the public eye. The POA (Prison Officers Association) had released a press statement complaining that Gartree's C Wing was being run under Sharia law and that non-Muslim inmates had been barred from showering naked or putting up topless pictures of women in their cells.

I don't ever recall being told what to wear during shower time but they were spot on about the atmosphere and the direction of travel. As usual, the Prison Service said there was 'no evidence to back up any of these claims about HMP Gartree'.

The prison staff were doing their best under the circumstances and many had become openly critical about their bosses at Prison Service headquarters. They were in despair at what had happened to their profession and the places in which they had invested years of their lives.

By now, new recruits had begun to fill the prison officer ranks. Like the rookie officer who was manhandled and stripped of the phone he'd just confiscated, many were young and lacked life experience. And yet they were still expected to enter volatile environments with little support. On one occasion, high up on the 3s landing, a 22-year-old female officer was pulled into a cell by a prisoner. With no staff around to assist, she might well have been raped if it hadn't been for the prisoners who had come to her aid after hearing her screams.

It wasn't just C Wing that had deteriorated: the whole prison was in turmoil. Gartree had a 'drug-free' wing which was infested with spice and prisoners with serious mental health issues. Almost every day, sometimes twice a day, an ambulance was called out to deal with a spice attack or an act of self-harm, resulting in routine suspensions of the regime, when we'd have to lock down so the emergency services could reach their destination.

When a regime starts to deteriorate, it sets in motion a chain of events that are felt throughout the prison. Instability takes up staff time, which provides space for more rule breaking and acts of violence, which creates a vicious circle as it further unsettles the regime. And not being able to retire to your living quarters without thinking you could be the next target means education and offending behaviour work are impacted. If rehabilitation becomes difficult for those who want to change, imagine how hard it is for those who are still at the pre-contemplation stage? You need to be able to step away from the heat, to have that time to dedicate to these things, but it is a non-starter when you are surrounded from all angles.

The increase in anxiety that this deterioration feeds means that it becomes impossible to think straight, to focus on your education, on making the progress through your sentence; instead, you're just focusing on getting through the day. – surviving. It's really unsettling for people: you're upstairs on your own, gangs are prowling the landings and if something were to happen, it's unlikely the staff are going to be able to do an awful lot about it.

The tension between Omar's group and some of my friends didn't prevent Omar from pestering me to train him, which I found strange. He'd stopped using the prison gym because of the music during sessions. Due to his fondness for violence and my hunch that it would be used to harm others, I always found an excuse to politely decline. Though I did continue chatting with him, if only out of intrigue.

With his cell wallpapered in Islamic procedures on ablution and a large aerial shot of Mecca, Omar, as far as he was concerned, had never been happier. In the same way that I felt freed from the negative aspects of my life, so did he. The violence that I'd gladly put behind me was simply a moral undertaking for Omar, utilised, although a little too enthusiastically, for the sake of his brothers and their perceived wider cause. No longer was he a drug addict who had to endure being ostracised by his own community or screwed over for what pittance he could muster. In his mind, he'd been accepted, had found meaning in his life and, perhaps, peace.

And why should my truth be any more sacred than his? I could just as well be indoctrinated. In fact, I know I am to some extent; we all are. But what if it's deeper than I realise and I'm the one who's still trapped? It's happened before. That's partly why I was sentenced to life.

But while Omar might have found personal gratification, others were paying for it. And that's because he was practising a cherry-picked form of Islam that had been created for personal rather than spiritual gains. Omar wasn't practising a faith, he was radicalised. Having never fully escaped his past, I believe he had simply transferred from one form of entrapment to another. Before making any fundamental alterations to his identity, Omar first needed to work on Richard Pratt.

It's not hard to imagine how a person's social or religious background could ease the transition to extreme ideological reasoning, particularly if there are shared cultural features or sense of injustice. But what makes an entirely different culture and moral code attractive to a northern, working-class bloke who, several years earlier, was kicking the shit out of the very people he would now die for? Richard Pratt, who fitted more comfortably into the bracket of a football hooligan on drugs prior to his conversion, and Wang Lei, who once told me he would willingly sacrifice himself for his country if his government required it, were great examples of people who had gifted themselves to a radically different ideology to the one in which they were raised. No one could seriously doubt that the groups with which they were affiliated weren't acting on the direction of an extremist idea. Anyone who beats up their neighbour for allegedly insulting their religious beliefs is extreme. Violent extremism is, after all, defined as using violence and intimidation to achieve one's aims.

The incidents I witnessed on C Wing showed me that the process of radicalisation is not something that can only happen in youth or over an extended period of time; with the right (or wrong) conditions, it can happen later in life too, and very quickly. You very much can teach an old dog new tricks – especially when the environment is drastically altered with the presence of violence and a radical idea (a solution) that seemingly provides sanctuary or belonging to susceptible men with limited opportunities.

Prisons are ideal places for the propagation of extreme ideas, even their creation. While there is a higher chance of coming into contact with extreme thinkers and those who prey on their peers for their own ends, the desire to escape or placate whichever demons haunt the mind is exacerbated by the myriad issues that plague prison environments. And when an alternative existence is presented, perhaps one with a doorway to a glorious world that exists beyond the physical, it's inevitable that some will wander down the rabbit hole to see what's there. And escape they might, but only to another prison. Rather than being loved by their brothers, the sad part is that men like Nadeem and Omar were essentially cannon fodder for an extreme ideology and those just seeking to make a few quid. These guys would have sacrificed themselves for their brothers, but to their brothers they were nothing more than useful, albeit very dangerous idiots.

In 2015, Michael Gove, the latest MP to take up the role of Justice Secretary, commissioned ex-prison governor Ian Acheson to lead an independent review into Islamic extremism in prisons, apparently much to the irritation of Michael Spurr, the chief executive of the National Offender Management Service.

The report was damning, highlighting a lack of oversight and direction from Prison Service leadership on the issue of extremism.

Quite possibly resulting from questions NOMS leadership were getting from further up the chain of command, on 22 April 2016, a group of senior officials arrived at Gartree. Their first stop: C Wing.

'We're here on behalf of Michael Spurr to investigate extremism in the prisons,' said their lead man.

'Nowt wrong on this wing, Gov,' said a prisoner while rolling his eyes. 'You know what the papers are like. It's all bollocks.'

He would say that, I thought. *He's one of them.* Little did the official know, he was talking to one of the main instigators.

Not that their visit made any difference in the short term. Less than a month afterwards, several prisoners were kicked up and down the landing and a young black lad had his back carved to pieces by a gang involving Nadeem and Aslam. The gashes were so deep, a female officer who tried to comfort him went into mild shock. Not long after that, Micky was finally attacked following another disagreement and someone else was tortured in his cell for allegedly not paying his debts. And all in the secure setting of a category B lifer establishment right in the centre of England.

There were certainly friendlier expressions of faith to be found at Gartree. Though, for me, while Bible studies at the multi-faith centre had been a welcoming sanctuary over the previous year, offering some great insights into faith, it had begun to lose its appeal on closer examination.

'How come you're no longer coming to church?' I asked a friend of mine.

'I'm not bothering,' he replied. 'They said I'm allowed to identify as gay but not live my life as gay.'

I had enormous respect for the chaplaincy team. They were kind and gentle people. It really did feel safe and welcoming there. But when all was said and done, just below the surface, they discriminated against their fellow human beings.

I shouldn't have been surprised that some in the prison chaplaincy still clung to the Old Testament decree that homosexuality is a sin. When an outside guest gave an hour-long speech maintaining that evolution was false and insisting the world was only a few thousand years old, he was received by the chaplaincy team like he'd brought news directly from the big man himself. Having personally witnessed the destructive impacts of intolerant ideas, the darker side of this seemingly harmless talk was not lost on me. Everyone's entitled to a world view that flies in the face of hundreds of years of conclusive scientific evidence but by allowing the multi-faith centre to run its services without any oversight, the prison was enabling irrational ideas to be transmitted to those under its care.

I came to find that, just as the Islamic faith was being distorted and put to use by those with criminal intentions, so the multi-faith centre was being used by those who had their own agendas. Religious practice and pastoral care have invaluable roles to play in prisons. They bring people together into communities and play a number of useful functions. And some of the finest people I've met are followers of faith. But poor state oversight of religion in prisons has enabled those with distorted interpretations to groom and soften the minds of some prisoners, complicating their rehabilitation and future reintegration.

I'd done well in the prison and had been told I could now 'consolidate my skills in a category C', in their terminology, which meant that the door was open for me to transfer to a category C prison.

I'd known I was due for a transfer for some time and I'd been looking at other prisons. I'd completed my course, which helped lower my risk, and had met the objectives that had been set for me by the authorities; now it was time to move on.

Even though they're lower-security prisons, some category Cs, owing to the fact that they contain prisoners who are serving relatively shorter sentences, are still quite volatile, something I was keen to avoid. I was either going to go back up north to HMP Humber, near Hull and consequently my family, or to another prison in the Midlands. But I'd heard about this prison called HMP Warren Hill, on the coast of Suffolk – a lot of my friends, other lifers, had gone there. And it sounded great. But they'd stopped taking standard lifers at that time, so I focused my mind elsewhere.

I was walking down the landing one day when a friend of mine called Errol passed me and said, 'Steve, don't tell no one, but I'm going to Warren Hill.'

'How you getting that?' I asked.

'I dunno – my probation officer just says I can go.'

Right. So I knocked on the door of my prison probation officer and said, 'He's going to Warren Hill. Can I go?'

He said, 'Give me a minute.' He came back out five minutes later and said, 'Yes, you can go.'

It may sound surprising but you have quite a bit of choice about which prison you can go to once you get to this point in the system. You have to justify it, of course – Humber was an easy one to reason because it was nearer my family. But it was always possible to pick the prison first and justify it afterwards. And even though Warren Hill was further from them, I knew it was a progressive regime and that it was the right prison for me. My family were on board with my choice – even though it would mean travelling further to visit. They told me I needed to do what was best for me.

And so on 24 November 2016, after dwelling in the same cell for over seven years, I was making the next step on my journey through the prison system. I was leaving with the hope that Prison Service headquarters were beginning to take the violence at Gartree more seriously. C Wing had been fitted with security cameras and I'd heard the prison had been earmarked to be placed within the remit of the Long Term and High Security Prison Estate (LTHSE), which meant it would get further resources to deal with its problems.

While I felt sad to be saying goodbye to my friends, many of whom were doing big sentences, I couldn't suppress another thought: *Thank God I'm getting out of here.*

But I would be left with a final reminder of why I'd grown to believe that violence was more than just a simple choice that people made. On the day I was leaving, someone had been the victim of a knife attack following an ongoing altercation between one of the gangs and a couple of black lads who had dared to challenge their authority. Making my way down the stairs with my belongings, I noticed blood from their skirmish was still drying on the steps and the handrail. Judging by the way it trailed down the stairway, it appeared that the gang's victim must have been fleeing the scene as they cut him up.

Violence, I thought to myself. *What a waste of life.*

PART V

Category C: HMP Warren Hill

CHAPTER 19

The Progression Regime

Overlooking Orford Ness on the south-east coast of Suffolk, HMP Warren Hill has an incredible sea view that stretches for miles into the distance. Every day you could observe yachts, ferries and giant tankers floating past on the horizon. On a stretch of land between the prison and the coastline, there is also a wildlife sanctuary where wild deer roam, marsh harriers glide over reed beds and rare species of bird blow in from the continent.

'If this was a house,' we used to comment as we gazed out of the window, 'the view alone would increase its values by thousands.'

Almost immediately below the wing was a falconry that held around thirty different birds of prey, including two bald eagles. Some of these birds were flown daily on the prison grounds by prisoners. Apart from the seagulls that nested on the flat roof above and woke me up at five o'clock every morning, I liked it. For the men who'd been locked deep inside the prison system for too many years, Warren Hill offered hope, an elusive notion across the prison system but one which was considered such an important aspect of rehabilitation that the word was inscribed on the wall at the prison's entrance. Considering the conditions at other prisons, Warren Hill was like paradise. The irony was that its regime and its progressive ethos had sprouted from the rubble of Chris Grayling's tenure.

In 2014, following over-hyped media coverage of several prisoners absconding from open prisons, Chris Grayling signed into force a law that prevented any prisoner with a history of absconding from being transferred to the open prison estate. For the indeterminate-sentenced prisoners who fell into this bracket, achieving freedom suddenly became a great deal harder, as they no longer had access to the open estate, which was the best means to demonstrate risk reduction, a precondition before full release on licence can be considered by the Parole Board.

As a result, HMP Warren Hill, a category C prison, brought into operation the Progression Regime, a closed prison environment that imitated the functions of an open prison. Even though it wasn't actually an open prison, it at least offered prisoners the opportunity to demonstrate the necessary reduction in risk for parole hearings.

The Progression Regime had three stages that a prisoner could work through if they could show good behaviour. The higher the stage you reached, the more access you had to enhanced facilities. Stage 3 prisoners, for example, could buy frozen meat and vegetables from a prison shop and cook it themselves in one of the kitchens on each wing.

'Residents', as we were referred to, remained unlocked until eight in the evening, in contrast to the customary five o'clock lockdown, and could go to the gym more often or take part in a variety of sports on a large field. In trying to replicate category D conditions, Warren Hill was like an open prison regime inside a closed prison, an arrangement that allowed the prisoners to mix more freely within their community.

Each prisoner was also paired up with a key worker, a prison officer whose role it was to conduct routine case-file updates and develop a trusting relationship with their assigned prisoner. And to try to help overcome the traditional 'us and them' barrier that existed across the prison system, Warren Hill staff wore blue polo shirts and trousers, rather than the standard black and white officer uniform.

Given where I'd been living for the previous ten years, I was more than relieved to find myself in an environment where violence was actively kept to a minimum. In theory, all prisons have a zero tolerance policy when it comes to violence, but unlike the prisons I'd been to, the managers at Warren Hill would immediately respond and remove violent prisoners from the prison. This gave the regime a better atmosphere, which was evident as soon as you walked through the gates.

It was also nice to bump into other prisoners whom I'd known for years, including many IPP prisoners, trapped in the system years beyond their tariffs. As the Progression Regime provided the means to prove yourself, it became the ideal place for IPP prisoners to make a genuine bid for freedom.

But the prison wasn't effective just because someone slackened the rules and called it 'the Progression Regime'. It was well led. Progressive-minded leadership was something I began to appreciate while at Warren Hill, and that was because the prison was headed by Sonia Walsh, a bold, ever-present and compassionate governor who had risen through the ranks of the prison system. A recent arrival herself, Sonia had quickly taken to Warren Hill's ethos and worked hard to preserve the ideas that underpinned its regime. This didn't mean she was soft. Far from it. Sonia would support you in your endeavours to change but if your behaviour put others at risk, you were swiftly removed from the prison.

'Is there a problem?' I once witnessed her say while facing up to a prisoner twice her size. 'That's not the sort of behaviour I would expect at Warren Hill.'

'No problem at all, Governor. Just passing by,' the prisoner said.

When someone doesn't compromise on their principles, their approach can sometimes seem impulsive and rude. Admittedly, it took time for me to warm to her. But after a while, I not only admired her style of leadership, I also grew to believe she was one of the best governors I'd ever come across. Sonia had a vision of how things ought to be and once that became clear, she was very likeable. Although not everyone agreed with her approach, they still knew their direction of travel. Her staff and senior leadership team were equally aware of their obligations. If she caught them slipping, she wouldn't hesitate to challenge them. Governor Walsh was firm when required but fair at the outset, which made all the difference.

Several months after I arrived at Warren Hill, a letter with familiar handwriting arrived through the post. It was from Jayne. Although we'd maintained sporadic contact as Jayne got on with her life, it had been over ten years since we last saw each other. Her letter explained that she wanted to visit me.

I knew she'd be nervous, just as I was, so I did my best to make her feel welcome. 'Come on, Jayne, let me show you the view,' I said as I led her to the back of the visits hall. 'That's where the birds of prey are kept.' I pointed to Warren Hill's falconry.

Jayne craned her neck to peer out of the window.

'Look, there's one there, sat on its perch.'

'Where?' replied Jayne as she squinted through her glasses.

The glasses were new – she hadn't worn them while we'd been together. I glanced at her while she strained to see the large falcon on its post. The lines near her eyes signified the passing of time between our encounters but the years had been kind. Jayne still looked great and had retained her beautiful smile. It was strange, because even though we hadn't seen each other in so long, I still felt like we'd just split up – the raw emotions came flooding back to me.

But this wasn't the time to address this. That time had long since passed. Before the visit, I'd noticed a surname I didn't recognise on the visits slip. Jayne was now married. She was a mum now, as well. It wasn't any of my business, of course. I was pleased that she was happy, as well as safe. After catching up with each other's lives, we hugged and then went our separate ways.

Heading back to my wing, I told myself everything was fine. Then, after I returned to my cell, I sat down, dropped my head on my desk and remained there. It had hit me harder than I thought it would. Seeing her again in the flesh brought home to me what I'd lost. Over the following days, I felt unmotivated, struggling to form a positive image of freedom – that thing that meant so much to me – without Jayne in my life.

In society, if you split with someone you love you can go for a drink, meet someone else, do something different. Life's distractions eventually take over and you ultimately move on. But in prison, where you cannot drown your sorrows or form a new intimate relationship, the feelings take longer to dissipate. It's like they're frozen in time.

That's what it had been like with Jayne – the feelings were still there. At one point during the visit, when she walked over to the canteen to get a coffee, I'd thought, *That could have been my wife.* But the truth was that she wasn't. She never would be. It was finished and I needed that sense of closure to move forward and look towards my own future. I was pleased that she had found someone and moved on, and through accepting this I was able to unfreeze my own feelings and move on too.

A short while later, in the spring of 2017, a friend of mine landed at Warren Hill. I'd met Ryan on the rugby pitch at Gartree and we'd hit it off immediately. Ryan had been sentenced 'at Her Majesty's pleasure' when he was just fifteen years old, which, in this instance, is a mandatory life sentence for those who are convicted of murder when under the age of eighteen. Ryan had practically grown up in prison. Yet he was incredibly polite, sociable and didn't seem to have a violent bone in his body. He was also a good example of what the prison system can achieve when a person has the will to change and develop themselves.

Shortly after arriving, Ryan became the distance learning rep at Warren Hill, a paid role which saw him promoting distance learning courses like those offered by the Open University. 'Surely it's about time you signed up for an OU course?' Ryan would pester me in an attempt to get me to apply myself more academically.

After some deliberation I eventually applied to do a businesss and management degree. It made sense given I'd reach the absolute limit on what prison education departments could offer me. Being a prisoner, however, didn't mean I would get the course for free. I would still have to apply for a student loan and accumulate a debt, repayable after earning over a set amount. But I felt that if one day I would be earning enough money to repay the loan, then I would be in exactly the place where I would want to be following release.

Around this time, Aaron, another prisoner who'd been sentenced at Her Majesty's Pleasure as a teenager, arrived at Warren Hill. He too had matured in prison and used his time wisely, writing and directing plays and receiving praise from the Justice Secretary, Michael Gove, for writing a book on a social model for prisons.

With his cell piled high with books, including on his toilet floor and windowsill, where they would get damp and mouldy, he reminded me of Jez, my friend back at Frankland. Someone else who believed that the journey was just as important as the destination. After we got to know each other, we took advantage of Warren Hill's relatively laid-back regime and spent hours discussing philosophy, politics, law and anything that came to mind.

If there is one crucial difference between a settled environment and a volatile one, it's the opportunities to engage in education and personal development without undue interference from your peers. In this respect, Gartree and Warren Hill were like night and day.

After Ryan had also persuaded Aaron to sign up to an Open University course, Warren Hill's library, which had a row of desktop computers installed for study purposes, became our home. That year, we completed a degree-level maths module and achieved 99 per cent in our final assignment, a result that would have been impossible without Ryan's help.

It was during those long hours in the library that the Head of Reducing Reoffending approached me. 'Steve, your name's been put forward as someone who might be interested in a project called Learning Together,' he said.

'I'm too busy,' I replied, while typing up an essay.

'It's run by two professors from Cambridge University,' he continued, eager to get the numbers up. 'They'll be bringing in students to collaborate with you guys.'

I continued typing, trying to look busy so he got the point: 'Seriously, I don't think I have time. I'm flat out with Open University stuff.'

'Look, just turn up next week, see what they have to offer, and if you're still not interested after that, then fine.'

CHAPTER 20

Learning Together

Dr Ruth Armstrong and Dr Amy Ludlow were the two Cambridge University academics promoting Learning Together, a research initiative that brought together prisoners and students into 'communities of learning'. Around twenty of us assembled in the visits hall as their audience and I was struck by just how good they were at communicating their ideas, though I also felt slightly intimidated by these super-bright visitors from what seemed like another planet.

But I would soon go on to discover that one of Learning Together's aspirations was to break down the barriers that they viewed as detrimental to social inclusion. And I learned that this objective would be achieved no more effectively than by the good-looking young chap sitting alongside Ruth and Amy on that first day.

'Hi guys, my name's Jack Merritt and I'm going to be the course co-ordinator at Warren Hill,' he explained in a posh accent and with a friendly smile, to a group of lifers listening intently.

Jack had been a student on a previous Learning Together course at HMP Grendon. His inspiration for his new role came from working alongside the prisoners there and observing what he considered their untapped potential.

Once everyone began asking questions, I set aside my own prejudice. 'I'm studying and have other commitments. I don't think I'll have time,' I declared.

'Time management,' Ruth responded promptly but politely, terminating my lazy excuse in an instant.

She was right. I just needed to adjust.

It was nothing new for academics and students to visit prisons – we'd seen it all before. The difference this time was that the Learning Together team was from Cambridge University, one of the most prestigious in the world. So Ryan, Aaron and I eagerly drafted our applications for what we thought would inevitably be a tough competition for the twelve spaces. Yet out of the 240 prisoners at Warren Hill, only around 14 applied for the pilot course. Cynicism and poor motivation are common among prisoners and often act as barriers to the uptake of these types of projects, but even I was surprised at the low turnout. Though it's quite possible that some of their reluctance was born out of the fact that projects involving outside guests tend not to have very long shelf lives, leaving some prisoners feeling left behind once the course is concluded.

Even Sonia Walsh was sceptical. 'So what are my boys going to get from this?' she asked.

Along with Ryan's and Aaron's, my application was successful, so I soon found myself engaged in what was the most academically stimulating experience of my sentence. The Learning Together course I'd enrolled on was named the Butler Law course, in memory of John Butler, a lawyer who'd died at a relatively young age. According to those who knew him, he came from a working-class background, was a compassionate human being and championed the underdog.

Our task was to produce legal advice guides in areas of law that were insufficiently accessible, in light of the rule of law principle that all law must be accessible, intelligible, clear and predictable.

We were split into groups with the university students, and Jack, Amy and Ruth gave us an overview of how laws are made, the hierarchy of the court system and the various types of law, followed by a lesson on legal research. We were then asked to choose a topic for our legal advice guides. Given that all the men residing at Warren Hill were Indeterminate Sentence Prisoners, my group decided on the idea of a guide on licence conditions for ISPs, the rules that govern behaviour while someone is on licence in society. Once my group had delegated tasks to each other, we then settled into completing the six-month course.

As someone who would eventually be living in the community under licence conditions, I found myself doing more than just researching content for our legal advice guide. I was familiarising myself with the implications of what I was reading. On eventual release, any breaches of these rules could see me being recalled to prison.

When I was in the library one day looking through the Prison Service instructions for licence conditions in the community, I came across a statement that brought home to me the eternal implications of my status as a life-sentence prisoner: 'Released lifers are subject to a life licence that remains in force for the duration of their natural life.'

All lifers are aware of this fact. But the potential impact of what this handful of words would mean in practice struck me profoundly. It made me think more deeply about my eventual release, the idea of freedom and what it would mean to be living in society as a UK citizen but under different rules to everyone else. In other words, despite being free from prison, would I ever be truly free while on a life licence? The answer, of course, was no. It began to play on my mind.

The work of academics is sometimes criticised for having little practical relevance to their subject matter but Learning Together was trying to overcome this with its presence on the ground. The approach offered the academics the opportunity to apply and adjust their theories, while the criminology and law students got the chance to meet the people behind their studies. As for us prisoners, we could absorb the hard-earned knowledge of Cambridge professors, judges, members of the legal profession and other guest lecturers who'd been slotted onto our timetable. We felt very privileged.

Following six months doing the course and creating our legal advice guides, an end-of-course conference was arranged to celebrate our achievements in the prison's visits hall. It was there, in April 2018, that I first met His Honour John Samuels QC, a retired Crown Court judge and ex-judicial member of the Parole Board. His role was to provide feedback on our legal advice guides alongside a panel of legal experts.

John had spent over four decades of his life administering the sharp edge of the law, undoubtedly making countless hardened criminals quiver in their boots in the process. Except John also represented what I later considered to be the most important aspect of the administration of justice: an appropriate sentence at the start, crucially accompanied by ongoing support and recognition once someone had come to terms with their sentence, committed to change and could evidence it. If there were more people like John Samuels sharing their time with the reviled, the world would be a much safer place.

Along with the exhibition of our work, the conference also provided the opportunity for some of the prisoners to showcase their talent. The music, artwork and poetry that was being created at Warren Hill was another great feature that was being established at the prison. It was a first glimpse for me into how powerful messages could be delivered across social boundaries using art. My friend Aaron gave a political speech that received a standing ovation. And another prisoner, Levi, showcased his impressive gift for poetry and was met with rapturous applause.

Like violence, art could stimulate strong emotions, but unlike violence, the most you could hurt someone was by challenging their perception on life. It appealed to me.

After some live music from a group of prisoners supported by musicians from Snape Maltings, which culminated in a round of applause, the conference ended on a high. Jack had a big smile on his face – he had just hosted his first successful course for Learning Together.

Following the conference, Ryan and I went back to our living quarters and reflected on our time with Learning Together.

'I don't think we'll see 'em again,' said Ryan.

'Who knows?' I replied. 'Maybe they've got what they need.'

We weren't expecting much else beyond our first year. But it wasn't long before Jack was back at the prison, this time with a list of pre-booked speakers on the different areas of law.

'I spoke to Ricky on Monday,' he said about a prisoner who'd recently been released. 'He's doing really well.'

'You heard from Ian?' we asked about another recently released prisoner who'd also been on the course.

'It's been tough getting hold of him. I think he's working but I'll keep trying,' Jack responded, without a hint of frustration.

Ryan and I knew how difficult it could be to positively

influence our peers and we had witnessed many enthusiastic professionals enter the prison system only to become demotivated and cynical within a matter of months. Yet Jack was not only passionate and undeterred; he made it look easy.

Now that we'd seen that their support was extending beyond the prison fence and Jack seemed to be playing a central role in this, it was clear that Learning Together weren't going anywhere soon.

One evening in May 2018, a conference took place on the Committee of the Prevention of Torture, led by Nicola Padfield QC (Hon), a professor of law at Cambridge University. I got chatting to a group of PhD students and I met Simon Larmour, who later joined the Learning Together team.

'I'm doing a PhD on childhood delinquency,' said Simon.

'Really? I used to be a delinquent,' I replied, self-mockingly.

My personal experience of how destructive juvenile delinquency can be to families and society meant the importance of his work was not lost on me. Simon was incredibly passionate about the subject so I offered to provide insights into my own childhood. After that, we began writing to each other about his PhD topic and struck up a friendship.

During the tea break, I began chatting to Nicola Padfield. That thought about the life licence had been niggling away at me, so I waited for my moment and just blurted it out.

'What do you think about the life licence?' I asked.

'I think it's abhorrent,' she replied, without missing a beat. 'In fact, I've written a paper on it.'

A sense of relief came over me. *Great,* I thought. *At least it's not just me, someone who'll be subject to one.*

I walked away from our brief conversation pondering the idea and later discussed it with friends. Everyone had mixed views. Some were unmoved and thought we deserved it, while others felt it was unnecessary to keep someone in a perpetual state of unease.

The vast majority of the men and women serving sentences have broken their social contract, the legal obligation to treat their freedoms responsibly. But although most offenders leave prison and eventually reacquire their full status as citizens after a limited period on licence, mandatory life-sentenced prisoners do not. Despite the fact that most eventually get released back into the community, they are never truly freed. Licence conditions are a set of rules an individual must follow in the community. They include restrictions on things like a person's free movement: where they must reside at night, who they can interact with, or where they can work, for example. Although licence conditions can be cancelled after ten years, a very difficult thing to achieve in any case, the licence itself can never be terminated. At any point in their life, the conditions can be reimposed or they can be recalled to prison. Life really does means life.

Without the evidence to demonstrate a significant reduction in risk, release by the Parole Board is impossible for ISPs, so I began to question the need for what seemed like an eternal punishment if someone could demonstrate beyond reasonable doubt that they are living as a law-abiding citizen and are no longer a risk to society. Although mandatory lifers have the lowest reconviction rates out of all prisoners released back into society, a period on licence makes sense, but only to manage offence-related risks and assist with their reintegration. If someone wants to commit a serious offence on licence, they'll do it anyway, regardless of the licence conditions, so the long-term benefits to the public are insignificant and the life licence serves only to have a detrimental psychological effect on the 'freed' lifer.

Are we really content with having lifers roaming the street, living among the free, if they are no longer a threat to society but potentially detached from it because of their status? Is that healthy? What are the benefits? These are the questions I began asking myself and debating at length with Ryan and Aaron. Surely it would be better to have a point – say, after ten years of trouble-free behaviour – at which a lifer could apply to the Parole Board to have their licence terminated. Imagine the outcome? It could motivate, inspire and offer people a real sense that they are truly reintegrated.

Unquestionably, something like this would need a tank just to get it to the gates of Parliament, so no chance of that happening anytime soon. But it got me thinking further about our country's approach to crime and punishment, while writing a letter to say thank you to the professor who'd unwittingly sustained my intrigue in the life licence. I thought about our government's view of freedom and how it contrasted with that of the emperors and senates who ruled during the age of the Roman Empire. Despite being a brutal period in the history of humankind, they understood the value of freedom to such an extent that they allowed slaves to pay for it or win it in the colosseum. And not all slaves were born into slavery, some were criminals, enslaved for crimes like murder. Yet here, in modern Britain, true freedom remains eternally unattainable for some of its citizens. I signed the letter and posted it.

★

Following the success of Learning Together's first Butler Law pilot course, a second followed soon after, and there were plans for us to become mentors to the people doing this course. Apart from our personal experiences of being on the wrong side of it, we still knew very little about the law in theory or practice. If Ruth and Amy wanted us to assist the next cohort of students, we needed to enhance our knowledge.

During a visit to Warren Hill's prison library, Ruth and Amy had noted the scarcity of law books, normally a vital resource. With the governor's blessing, they decided to create another library and a space to deliver the next course, opposite the education department. A couple of months later, after Jack and Amy had bruised their forearms carrying boxes full of old and new law books donated by Oxford and Cambridge Universities, Warren Hill had its first law library.

As the summer of 2018 came around, Aaron, who'd recently directed a play called *The Long Road Home* at Warren Hill, which had been well received by the governor, had begun recruiting and looking for ideas for another performance. I had no real plans to get involved but since I'd been thinking about the idea of freedom, I thought about writing a scene about a prisoner attempting to achieve their freedom but never truly succeeding because of his life licence. Then I considered how much I disliked the drab setting of prison environments. So instead, I decided to write about a slave in Roman times fighting to win his freedom. Once I'd finished, I doubted its potential, buried it under a pile of papers and thought nothing more of it.

In the meantime, the prison was holding an official opening night for the law library. Many guests were going to be present, like the England and Wales Law Commissioner, David Ormrod, and John Samuels QC, who was going to cut the ribbon along with Sonia Walsh. Prior to the opening ceremony, Jack was holding a presentation downstairs in the multi-faith centre about the advice guides we had created on the first Butler Law course. Following tea, we all turned up in anticipation of who we'd be meeting.

'Right, guys,' said Jack. 'Just give your presentation on the legal advice guides you created. That'll be great.'

Usually, we'd just sit there while Jack or others praised our efforts, so the sudden realisation that we would have to work a little harder for our glory caught us off guard. To be fair, Jack had asked us to put something together but his request had somehow slipped under the radar. I'd been busy with my Open University work and writing the scene. We should have been better prepared.

As the guests started piling into the multi-faith centre, some of the lads started becoming nervous. It was contagious and soon spread among our group.

'I'm OK, thanks,' said one of the guys. 'Someone else can do it.'

'I'm not doing it,' another followed up.

Jack tried to reassure everyone: 'You can all say something. It won't take more than five minutes each.'

I turned to Aaron, who was trying to quickly scribble something down on a piece of paper. 'Do you want to do something?' I asked. 'You got something lined up?'

'No,' he responded. 'Why don't we both do something?'

'What like?'

'We could talk about law and justice,' Aaron said convincingly. 'Like two philosophers having a debate.'

'Yeah, yeah, good idea.' Then I thought about it . . . 'No, no, sod that! What do we know about law and justice? Just do a speech like you did last time.'

While waiting for the governor to arrive, the guests sat there watching us debate anxiously about who was going to do what. By now, Jack could tell we weren't going to produce what he had obviously invited the guests to see. I could see him talking to Ruth, whose face was like thunder.

In the end, some of us muddled through the presentations. It wasn't our best performance but Jack covered most of the cracks and, as usual, one of Levi's poems revitalised the moment. Then we all piled upstairs and officially opened the law library.

The next time Jack came to Warren Hill there was no handshake and his customary smile was replaced with a nod as the box he was carrying hit the desk a little harder than usual. Sensing his disapproval, a few of us mentioned the presentation, clumsily attempting to justify ourselves.

'Preparation, guys,' Jack said brusquely. 'All you need to do is prepare.'

There was no disagreeing. We'd become too comfortable. We had produced the legal advice guides so we should have been able to present something of worth. But Jack wasn't the type to let things fester. This was just his way of saying fix up – so we did.

Following the success of Aaron's first play, a Ministry of Justice official had procured the funds to purchase a portable stage for the prison and Sonia Walsh, inspired by what she'd seen, hired a professional performing arts team to help develop the next project. Red Rose Chain was a theatre and film company based in Ipswich and owned by Jo Carrick, a director and playwright.

For the first official workshop with Jo and her husband Dave, Aaron had persuaded around twenty lads to turn up. After everyone left the exercise yard to attend, I hung back and relaxed in the sun. I didn't fancy it. But then I could feel a nagging sense of doubt getting the better of me.

I eventually strolled in late. And after catching the back end of the warm-up session, which was followed by improvising a few scenes from *Romeo and Juliet*, I discovered that I loved it. Prancing about while displaying a façade was clearly still part of me.

A week later, I was in Aaron's cell discussing potential ideas for the next play after another meeting had failed to come up with anything compelling. I'd not mentioned anything about the Roman slave scene I'd jotted down but the ongoing suggestions of performing something about prisons and gang violence was putting me off. I'd seen enough prison violence not to want to start re-enacting it.

'I've wrote a scene,' I said. 'Wanna hear it?'

Aaron nodded.

As I talked through the scene, it was like we were there, sitting in the same field as the slaves two thousand years ago. No doubt our predicaments enabled us to empathise with the two characters I'd written about.

Aaron loved it. The Roman stuff on its own was never going to cut it so we decided to track that story alongside the journey of a prisoner in modern times fighting for freedom but never quite achieving it because of the life licence. By interlocking the scenes, we could show the link between the two stories and highlight the contrast between ancient and modern thoughts on freedom.

'Even better,' I said, 'Why don't we have the chap in prison reading the story of the Roman slave from a book?'

Aaron smiled.

Having had no previous experience in scriptwriting, I was still hesitant, but by sharing the story with Aaron, I'd practically sealed my fate.

Now that I'd committed to writing something for a play, I was back in the prison library again, researching Roman history and typing away. On the computer next to me was a skinny guy with a rough complexion. I'd noticed him visiting the library over the previous few months but after I'd seen him bang the desk and shout at his computer screen a couple of times, I got the impression he was either dabbling in drugs or lacked emotional control. Either way, I avoided interaction with him. But now it was unavoidable.

'Excuse me, mate,' he asked. 'How do you spell "absurdity"?'

'Just type in the nearest spelling then run spellchecker over it,' I replied with a glance before turning back to my screen. I would have left it at that but in that glance I'd noticed something on his screen.

'What's that you're writing, mate?' I asked.

'I'm writing a screenplay,' he responded. 'That's what I do. I'm a writer.'

'Oh, yeah?' I replied, pleasantly taken aback. 'So what are you writing?'

'It's about a shoplifter . . .' he started, before going on to explain the plot and telling me, 'I'm gonna rewrite the screenplay. Me sister's already contacted someone outside. It's gonna be big.'

His name was Max and suddenly I'd found a scriptwriter and someone else I could speak to about this form of art that I knew very little about. From that moment, we hit it off. Though I did think he'd be better off learning how to spell before taking on the slightly more challenging task of writing a revolutionary screenplay from a prison library.

'We're doing a bit of drama in the multi-faith centre tomorrow afternoon,' I explained. 'Why don't you come with me and try my scene?'

CHAPTER 21

The Citizen

Breaking into small groups, we took turns to see what we could come up with for what was, at that point, the basic structure of a scene involving two slaves in Roman times.

After loading turnips onto a cart, Gaius drops wearily to the floor and looks at his father. 'Why do you work so hard?'

Leo wipes the sweat from his brow. 'Son, the work of slaves is the foundation of this empire.'

'Then without us, there wouldn't be an empire.'

Leo shakes his head.

'But the Wooden Sword, it's a way, Father, for slaves to win their freedom.'

'The only freedom to be found in the Colosseum for a slave is death, and a gruesome one at that, while the people of Rome clap and cheer.'

'But I'm tired of being a slave,' protests Gaius as he rises to his feet. 'What makes me so different?'

'You cannot defy the gods, Gaius,' his father shouts. 'Or your place in life.'

Gaius cries out rebelliously. 'I defy the gods. I defy all rules . . .' Then, realising he may have exceeded his limits, he sits back down, drops his head, and relents. 'And I'm hungry.'

Leo looks at Gaius sympathetically and tells him to rest while he fetches water.

Gaius steals a turnip and sneaks off to eat it.

The scene culminated in Leo sacrificing himself to save his son from the wrath of the centurions, after which Gaius swore to avenge his father's death before fleeing to begin his destiny as a gladiator.

What began as a practice session to try out a humble scene ended two hours later with a group of men feeling a peculiar sense of purpose. Somehow, we'd released a bit of magic and everyone felt committed to making something work. But no one was more excited than Max.

'I want to write the next scene. Let me write the next one,' he persisted as we all left the multi-faith centre on a high.

The next Learning Together course was not due to start until late autumn but that didn't mean we could rest on our laurels. Ruth, Amy and Jack had plans. We were not only helping to deliver the next course; we were involved in redesigning the activities that would help instil the learning. And now that the law library was fully functioning, Amy and Jack decided that they would personally teach us an introduction to law.

Although we'd touched on law during the first course, and Aaron and I had already sneaked a couple of shelves' worth of law books back to our cells, having a Cambridge University doctor of law teach us alongside Jack took things up a level. Without a doubt, trying to extract the binding part of a legal precedent – in other words, differentiating between the *ratio decidendi,* 'the reasons for a decision' made in a previous case, and the *obiter dictum*, things 'said in passing' – was challenging for us novices. But the stuff we were learning about the UK constitution gave us fascinating insights into how power is created and distributed in our country.

Terms like Parliamentary Sovereignty (the principle that makes Parliament the supreme legal authority in the UK) and the Separation of Powers (the principle that attempts to safeguard the division of power between the legislature, the executive and the judiciary) had meant nothing to us previously. But now we understood why we have an uncodified constitution, why EU law has no effect without an Act of Parliament and why, at the end of each day, Amy and Jack could walk out of the front gates and we, barring a miracle, could not leave until at least the minimum terms of our life sentences were spent.

To assist with our learning, Amy brought in a box full of books titled *The Rule of Law* by Tom Bingham which, among other things, broke down the history and development of UK law. Our task was to analyse each chapter and draft our insights after each session. Gradually, with their expertise and resources, we began to develop a sense of place in the world and, despite our lowly positions in the hierarchy of life, a sense of pride.

This was a time that I look back on now with great fondness. Being in a progressive prison and learning with Jack and these incredible people was a great education for us. And not just in the technical legal knowledge they were sharing with us. Their values of community, kindness and being non-discriminatory were passed on to us – and the way that they communicated their ideas, too, was a revelation. Everyone was welcome there, no matter who you were, what your sentence was, the colour of your skin or your beliefs.

Learning Together would also invite all sorts of people to come and speak with us – lawyers, judges, people from all walks of life. Some of them would believe keenly in the effectiveness of prison and we'd debate with these people who offered different perspectives. It almost became a networking opportunity too: many of the people I met during this period would go on to help me later down the line – even when I was eventually released. It was an enlightening time, which felt like it opened up a whole world of possibility.

Back in the multi-faith centre, we'd been working on the next scene for the play. After making his way to Rome and being taken on by Porcius, a legendary trainer, Gaius finds himself in the vaults of the Colosseum waiting for his next fight.

Another prisoner called Pablo, a larger-than-life black lad with powerful vocals and fearless acting skills, had turned up to this session to play Gaius's rival – Pacideanus.

While Gaius was warming up for his fight, Pacideanus had noticed his presence.

'Black dog! Black sheep! Black day! Your fate awaits you, Gaius,' roared Pacideanus while pacing up and down and swinging his sword. 'I've killed fifty men, six bulls and two lions. You should go back to farming where you belong, picking turnips for your master.' Pacideanus then turns to Gaius. 'Or did you fail at that too? I heard your father died like a goat for your sins.'

In the blink of an eye, Gaius jumps up and places his sword against Pacideanus's neck, who is unable to move. 'Do not mention my father,' warns Gaius.

'Gladiators,' Porcius shouts as he steps in and gently removes the sword from Pacideanus's neck, 'this is not the time, or place.'

Gaius backs away and sits down.

Porcius joins him. 'You will never triumph while anger controls you.'

'But the memory of my father still burns me.'

'It is only in life that you can honour the dead. You must keep yourself alive until you are ready. Pacideanus is too strong for you now. I can strengthen your sword arm, but only you can strengthen your mind.' Porcius places his hand on Gaius's shoulder. 'Win your thoughts and you will win your freedom.'

Our main character, Gaius, was in a dark place but we knew his escape could only come from within, by facing up to his demons, rather than using physical force to achieve his aims. We were gripped, almost like we were there with Gaius, all those years ago.

While our group had been developing the Roman story, Aaron had been writing the script for a lifer journeying through his sentence in the present day. With a scene in hand, we all turned up to a session being held by Jo, who'd recently brought in her full cast to act out a scene from *Romeo and Juliet*, her latest show at her theatre.

But we had a problem. Aaron's ability to write about complex subjects led to a dense script that was hard to memorise and deliver for those who lacked experience, which was just about all of us. Furthermore, Aaron had come up with the idea of writing additional political scenes to intertwine with the other two stories.

Aaron's idea not only complicated the scriptwriting but it meant we now had to find more actors. We had a mountain to climb but the rewards had the potential to greatly outweigh the effort. Left largely to our own devices by the prison, this was a rare opportunity to talk about our world, the impact of politics on our lives and the human side of prisoners.

With unrest on the streets outside Parliament due to austerity, our prime minister was mindful of the impact this could have on the next election. His adviser was in no doubt about the required approach.

'It is time for a diversion strategy, one that taps into the fears of our nation. And what better way to get the people on side than to exploit crime and disorder,' thundered the adviser while leaping to his feet. 'Let's enliven the press, distract the people and focus their attention on the real enemy [criminals].'

In the meantime, the cast had congregated in the law library to discuss the storyline. Jo and her team were also present. Aaron was unsure about the need for the play to focus so intensely on the idea of one group of people, those on life licence, being the sole benefactors of compassion. Instead, he proposed the idea that all criminals should be treated the same and forgiveness offered universally.

'What you trying to say, we should forgive nonces too?' came the response when some of the group contemplated the implications.

'Yeah, fuck that!' said another. 'Why should rapists be forgiven?'

The idea wasn't going down too well but Aaron stood his ground as a heated debate broke out.

'Think about it, we're all hated anyway,' came the opinion from another. 'Some people believe if you take a life, they should throw away the key.'

'Or be hung,' someone else pointed out.

'Yeah, but fucking nonces deserve to die.'

How could we write a play that calls for compassion for lifers if we could not even find it in ourselves to forgive others for their crimes? What made us think that we were so special, particularly when we knew we were at the bottom of the pile by any standards?

'But unlike other criminals, our licence does last for ever,' I added while others threw in their opinions.

'It's so interesting listening to your debates, guys,' said Jo.

'Why don't you put this debate in the play, exactly how you're having it now?' suggested Katie, Jo's assistant, while the group continued to exchange verbal blows.

Crimes against women and children invoke a deep sense of unease because most people have a natural tendency to protect women and children, not hurt them. Personally, I've always considered the perpetrators of such acts to be among the most spineless. In prisons, this widely shared view shapes the social hierarchy. So long as they are not protected by the Islamist brotherhood, those who have committed such acts can count themselves lucky if they receive so much as a glance from someone further up the uncodified chain of command. If a bit of common decency is hard to achieve, then imagine the type of resistance that can emerge when an idea like forgiveness is raised.

But now that Aaron's point was out in the open, it could not be ignored. How could we alone expect forgiveness? Given we'd all cast a stone or two, reason implied that the principle was either universal or it failed altogether. For sure, we weren't on the cusp of arguing for the immediate release and a big soft hug for those who continued to hurt the vulnerable. Our compassion was about understanding, so that those who had committed offences could be given the space to move away from crime and towards a life of relative normality.

Now that we had broadened the scope of our final message, reason again dictated that there was no point in marketing the virtues of a principle if we couldn't put it into practice ourselves. Even within our own little group, we were faced with the practical challenges of the prison hierarchy and our own prejudices. Warren Hill did contain a few prisoners who were serving sentences for crimes against women and so did our group, which created a degree of awkwardness as certain fringe members muttered their reluctance to work alongside these participants.

But as prisoners, we understood that if you oppress people, stigmatise them or push them to the margins of your community, then they stay there, detached from 'your' community. It is the place where self-worth dissipates and resentment festers, creating the type of darkness that makes people less willing or able to self-reflect or engage with professionals, and it increases their chances of reoffending. So if we truly disagreed with crimes being committed against women and children, or anyone for that matter, then we had to swallow our feelings of revulsion and vengeful urges so that the perpetrators of those crimes could drift in from the wilderness and hopefully get on with the work of understanding their motivations. For us to take a hypercritical stance against 'the unpopular' would be to actively risk increasing the chances of them committing the very offences we supposedly don't want them to.

Consenting to a broader type of social tolerance also stemmed from my experience of what can happen when high levels of intolerance enter your world. For too many years I had watched how detached, self-serving groups ripped the soul from their community. Who'd want to sustain that? If tolerance, reason and humanity had not quite filtered through to every section of society, that didn't mean we couldn't implement it in our tiny space on a windswept coastline in Suffolk. It did not matter if you were pink, old, Muslim, black or Tibetan; if you were serious and wanted to contribute positively to the show, the door was open. We didn't leave anyone out.

Well, at least we thought we hadn't.

'Why don't you guys have any female characters in your script?' Jo asked us.

Aaron, Ryan and I looked at each other. 'There's no women in the prison.'

'I hope you don't mind,' said Jo, 'but I've wrote a scene for the Roman story and it has a girl in it.'

'But we don't have anyone to play her,' we responded.

Jo glanced towards her assistant, Katie.

So two scenes containing this female character would soften the edges to what was otherwise going to be a storyline dominated by men pumped full of testosterone and screaming at each other.

'Check out this scene, Ste,' said Max, waving it around. 'Man's gonna rewrite screenplay.'

By now, I'd discovered that my initial thoughts about whether Max was on drugs or just lacked emotional control were slightly wide of the mark: it was actually a combination of both. But Max was very gifted, not just with his writing but also as an actor.

Max had written what became known as 'The bath scene', which centred around two Roman senators relaxing in a Roman bath and discussing their concern about the growing admiration for Gaius among the citizens of Rome. In short, they wanted rid of him.

'We must crush the one they call Gaius, once and for all.'

'You do not adhere to the correct political procedures?'

'I do so. But in this case, I have made an exception.'

'Made?'

'Plans are already afoot,' revealed Augustus.

Throughout the summer months, Jack and Amy continued their visits, teaching us the basics of law and helping us to prepare for the next course. With a carrier bag full of M&S food, Jack would often turn up on his own or sometimes accompanied by a lecturer or a professional in the field of law, eager to impart their knowledge. It might sound strange to talk this way about M&S food that many people take for granted every day on their lunch break but we hadn't had food like this for years: it was like tasting freedom.

By now, we were beginning to see Jack as one of the lads, someone we could talk with about almost any subject. But he was always professional, too. Jack was super-smart. Having a master's degree from Cambridge University meant he could get a job practically anywhere, yet he was spending time with prisoners. It showed to us that he was serious about what he was doing. He was the real deal. Despite his young age, he'd become a mentor figure to us.

'There's something special about him,' Ryan would often remark.

Jack wasn't just clever, cool and handsome, though; he had a way with people. He had a natural ability to make even the most dejected prisoner feel valued. Prisons can be cruel places, where the weak are routinely trodden over and oppressed by their outwardly stronger peers, but Jack, along with the Learning Together team, was helping to lift the spirits of anyone fortunate enough to meet him. Self-worth and self-efficacy are scarce commodities in prisons, yet vital for personal growth and developing a can-do attitude that allows you to look beyond the immediate confines of a prison environment.

To show our appreciation, Ryan and I always cleaned and prepared the law library before they arrived to take a session. It was the least we could do.

As we reached crunch time on preparing the play, Aaron had received news about his HMP (Her Majesty's Pleasure) tariff review, which can sometimes result in a sentence reduction of up to two years. Aaron had done everything he could to be a positive force within the prison: he had thrown himself into education, into working with Learning Together and driving the arts at Warren Hill. He was actually doing things to help rehabilitate his fellow prisoners, and you don't get much better than that. Yet his appeal was rejected, which was a real kick in the teeth for him. The news hit him so hard that it left him seriously demotivated, which meant we might no longer have his full attention for the rest of the play.

In fact, the news had a profound effect on Aaron, sending him into a deep depression, and it wasn't hard to see why. He was non-violent, he'd changed his life in prison, and it left me wondering what more can a man do? The expectations of those convicted of a crime are to go to prison, serve their punishment and rehabilitate. Yet when people do that, it can still be extremely difficult to get recognition for it.

The law in prison has the opportunity to offer people hope. If the law is strong enough to show that if you do the right thing, you'll be rewarded, then that offers hope to prisoners. It offers the possibility of rehabilitation. But if you're just left with arbitrary interpretations of the law, as I believe was the case with Aaron, then it runs the risk of demotivating people, as some will inevitably think, *Well, what's the point in changing, then?* Good law offers hope and I don't believe the current system supplies enough of that.

★

I invited my friend Daz to join us on stage, to play the Roman emperor in a scene where Gaius wins his freedom. Daz had been the first Prison Council chair at Gartree and I had a feeling he would enhance our group with his presence.

Prior to the finale, there was just one more scene to establish, an assassination attempt on Gaius at the request of the Roman senators. It was while I was writing this scene in my cell that I appreciated the wider benefits of the visualisation techniques I'd acquired during my years of doing Brazilian jiu-jitsu. It was ideal for stage choreography – for the fight scene we were going to stage. It presented a few challenges, not least the need for fight-worthy swords and the ability to use them. Fortunately, Daz was a builder by trade so was able to make some wooden swords in the prison workshop. And Jo hired a fight choreographer. A few weeks later, our fight scenes were perfected and the multi-faith centre was full of cast members eagerly clashing swords and feigning injuries.

As for Gaius, he survived the assassination attempt from his training partner, Celadus. But rather than take revenge, Gaius let Celadus flee.

'Why did you spare him?' complained Porcius as he watched Celadus escape from the building.

Gaius turned to Porcius. 'Have you forgotten what it was like to be a slave?'

Finally, our character was growing.

With only a few weeks to go before the full performance of the play, now dubbed *The Citizen*, we set about building the stage in the multi-faith centre and ordering costumes. Jo had hired suits for the political scenes and invites had been sent out to the Ministry of Justice, which meant some important guests would be in attendance.

'Don't let me down, boys!' warned Governor Walsh, with a rare hint of edginess in her voice.

'Don't worry, Governor,' we assured her. 'We'll deliver.'

But behind the scenes, our problems persisted. Aaron had stopped functioning at his normal level and he no longer wanted to act in the play.

'We need you, Aaron!' Max and I pleaded. 'We don't have anyone else.'

'It's not a problem,' Aaron responded casually. 'We can find someone else.'

'Who?'

A few days later, Aaron turned up with his solution. 'He can do it,' he said.

Standing next to Aaron was a scruffy-looking prisoner who looked like he'd just fallen out of the sky.

'Aaron, we can't use him. He looks like he's on fucking spice!'

As we entered the final week, the situation was becoming desperate. The cast had grown to around twenty members and the professional actors had been attending more frequently, yet we still only had two-thirds of the script.

In one final push, Max and I took turns speaking to Aaron after we'd come up with an idea for the script. Somehow, we managed to light a spark and Aaron was suddenly back in the fold. Against all the odds, within a matter of days, we were back on track.

'It's like treacle, guys,' Jo warned us while we transitioned through each scene of the play. 'You need to speed up. You don't want the audience falling asleep.'

On the night before the show, in October 2018, with barely an hour left of the final practice session, we'd reached the concluding Roman scene, which was a sword fight between Gaius and Pacideanus. Daz was on stage, dressed as an emperor, looking every bit the part as two Pretorian guards stood either side of him. The gladiators clashed below. As eight men jostled for position, trying to fit into a tiny space, the tension increased. Then, out of nowhere, an exchange of words erupted between Aaron and Daz, resulting in Daz throwing his costume to the floor and walking out of the building.

'That's it,' he snapped. 'I'm finished! Find someone else.'

Everyone looked at each other as if to say, 'Shit!'

'It's all right,' I said confidently. 'I'll chat to him tomorrow. He'll be fine.'

The next morning, the cast and crew congregated in the multi-faith centre. With the windows blacked out with old bed sheets, an artificial lighting system installed and enough chairs to seat over 70 guests, the stage looked just like it was nestled in the corner of a cosy little theatre. And now we had a professional guitarist (a serving prisoner) and a PlayStation 2 wired up to some loudspeakers, we could seal the edges of *The Citizen* with some music and well-timed sound effects.

But it turned out that Daz wasn't fine. Despite the fact that he was meant to play two roles and had memorised a rather lengthy piece of script, he wasn't budging.

'Daz, please,' begged Ryan.

'No!'

Even Jo went to see him.

'No!'

Then the governor.

'No!'

This time, with no emperor and only two hours to go, we really were in trouble. And everyone felt it. We sat in silence for a while, pondering what to do. Then, for the last time, our show was saved.

'I'll do it!' said Levi.

He'd looked over the script the previous night and memorised most of it. 'The rest,' he said, he would, 'improvise.'

It was a shot of adrenaline for us. We fired back up and delivered the product of six months' worth of blood, sweat and tears.

As the audience sat watching the emperor seated at the centre of the stage, from the back of the theatre tumbled Pacideanus after being viciously wounded by Gaius. Down to the sand he crashed while Gaius stood over him with his sword.

'Raise your hand, Pacideanus. Beg for your life and receive mercy from the crowd . . .'

'Black dog. Black sheep. Black day,' he groaned in a fading voice. 'I am Pacideanus the mighty. I do not beg for mercy.'

Gaius raises his sword. 'Then you will die!'

'Do not falter like your father,' taunts Pacideanus.

Hearing his father being mentioned during the heat of his fury, Gaius stops. As the sun beats down and the mob screams for blood, he contemplates the strength of his honour. He looks to the sky. 'What would he think?'

'Finish me,' mouths Pacideanus.

Gaius raises his sword, then throws it to the ground before turning to the baying crowd. 'Mercy is mighty! Forgiveness is just!' he shouts.

After a moment or two, the crowd join in. 'Mercy is mighty! Forgiveness is just!'

Gaius had truly won their hearts.

We couldn't have Gaius winning his freedom from slavery purely through the spilling of blood. Fortunately, the emperor didn't mind either and after Gaius had knelt on one knee, out came the Wooden Sword to mark his freedom. Then a speech to the nation about compassion for all brought *The Citizen* to a close with a standing ovation.

Daz, who had watched the show alongside Jack and Simon, climbed on stage at the closing moments to humbly express his remorse for dropping us in it at the last minute and missing out on the play, for which he received his own round of applause.

As we slowly returned the room to being a multi-faith centre from its incarnation as a theatre and packed away our costumes and makeshift props, the sense of accomplishment was overwhelming. Despite the odds being stacked against us, we had succeeded on so many levels.

A short while later, we also discovered that our voices had spread a little further than just the eyes and ears of those who attended that day. Libby Purves, a journalist who had attended the play, wrote a piece for *The Times* newspaper about *The Citizen*. Given our last-minute challenges, it wasn't surprising that she noted that it was 'artistically a bit of a jumble . . . But gripping, too.'

Libby Purves' piece even referred to the 'life licence' and its eternal existence. Somehow, that initial seed of thought I'd had, had managed to reach a far wider audience than I could ever have imagined.

CHAPTER 22

Life Imitating Art

In November 2018, Aaron, Ryan and I began our mentoring roles with the launch of the next Butler Law course. Around the same time, a separate Learning Together event saw a large contingent of university students fill the multi-faith centre. One of the themes was related to the theory of desistance. I had heard this term in passing before but never outside the orbit of Learning Together.

Unlike rehabilitation, which is said to be a process that an offender is 'put through' by the system, or that is 'done to' an offender, desistance is the process of development through which a person moves away from crime or criminalisation. It is neither an event nor an 'intervention'. While it is often thought that desistance (like recovery from addiction) comes from within, it is also strengthened by external support mechanisms. Although I'm certain there was an 'event' that initiated my abstinence from violence, when I applied desistance theory to my notion of what may have been occurring over the years, it seemed to fit more appropriately than the idea that I was being rehabilitated by the state.

The term rehabilitation seems to have lost its way over the years, perhaps by showing poor returns or, from the prisoner's perspective, by the system making demands that are impossible to satisfy. Work as hard as you can to change your life around and even back it up with concrete evidence, even then, you will never hear the words, 'Well done, you're rehabilitated.' But you can very easily and very often hear the opposite message, even in response to hearsay evidence of a minor rule infringement.

While the system places the burden of reducing risk on the prisoner, most of the means of doing so are owned by the state. This is why prisoners can be so easily demotivated when they are refused release or progression to open conditions due to a lack of resources (i.e. offending behaviour courses or education programmes), rather than a lack of motivation or evidence of change.

Perhaps the prisoner Red, played by Morgan Freeman in the film *The Shawshank Redemption,* was on to something when he sat before his parole board and remarked, 'Rehabilitated? It's just a bullshit word.'

Ironically, he was freed.

'I've just been speaking to Aaron,' said Max as he rushed into my cell. 'We think you should direct the next play. What you saying?'

'Let's see what everyone else says first,' I replied. 'Someone else might wanna do it.'

'Fuck that, Steve,' cried Max. 'I can't be directed by anyone else. We can do it. I can be your co-director.'

The thought of me and Max wrestling over the scenes ran across my mind. 'Nah, not two of us. That wouldn't make sense.'

'All right, then, just you direct.'

Aaron's magic and the experience of *The Citizen* had helped release artistic talent that many of us never knew we had. We'd caught the bug.

'OK, I'll do it,' I said. 'Any ideas?'

The year is 1704, and Devilfish, the most feared pirate captain to ever sail the high seas, is aboard his ship, The Albatross, *in the Caribbean Sea. After his daring raid to steal treasure had resulted in the capture of his vice-captain, Jon Van Hepper, Devilfish was determined to rescue him from his holding cell at Port William, where he was being held by the Spanish.*

So, pirates it was, and off we went to join them on an adventure that would lead to another six months of plotting and character building at HMP Warren Hill.

We named this one *The Albatross*, after the pirate ship. Max would play its captain, Devilfish, and I his vice-captain, Jon Van Hepper. Our strongest actors were given the major parts, with Daz particularly keen to make amends for missing out last time. But as usual, we still had our work cut out.

'You two think it sounds better than it is,' mocked Levi while listening to me and Max boasting as we read out the script in the library.

While we half expected it, it wasn't a good sign. Levi had been one of our strongest actors.

A few days later, after Max had caught Levi in a better mood, he placed one of our best pieces of the script on the table next to him. Without looking at it, Levi picked it up and filed it half-heartedly among his paperwork.

In the meantime, Governor Walsh, our biggest advocate, had moved on to manage another establishment and the new governor, Dave Nicholson, had begun his tenure at Warren Hill. To our benefit, he was equally enthusiastic about performing arts and made a pledge to continue supporting their development at Warren Hill. And with our request for financial support settled, Jo was back at the prison to provide a hand.

Now I had just one more matter to iron out: Max. He was committed but his tendency to drift off was a risk. I needed an insurance policy.

'Max!'

'What?' he replied.

'You see that empty cell opposite mine?'

'Yeah?'

'Go get your stuff. You're moving in.'

I needed Max as much as he needed me, so keeping him close would allow me to get the best out of him.

While Max and I set about trawling through every library book we could get our hands on that covered the dawn of the eighteenth century, Jack had sourced us a number of documents related to the same period. With the court cases, notable hangings and contemporary papers on the use of capital punishment for pirates he sourced, we soon had enough material to infuse some historical authenticity into our play.

Just as we had with the Roman slaves, as Max and I immersed ourselves in the golden age of piracy, we felt an eerie connection to some of the characters we studied. Their lives were exciting but harsh. After long voyages that were filled with danger, disease and deceit, they ended either dramatically with an overindulgence in plunder or, more commonly, with the pirates losing their lives, sometimes by hanging.

In one little book I discovered in the library, I stumbled across a story of some pirates who had been sentenced to hang in the late 1700s, yet rather than be swung from the noose, the English monarch, King Charles II, gave them a Royal Pardon, as they had been in possession of a rare map which they had stolen from the Spanish. It got me thinking about how to end the performance.

From this tale, I determined too that the real reason Devilfish wanted to help his vice-captain escape was because he was the only person who knew the whereabouts of a map. And not just any old map but a rare book of charts called the Spanish Corpora.

Around this time, Aaron and I attended a music event, one of many such arts and charity events held at Warren Hill. Also there was George Vestey, the High Sheriff of Suffolk. George was a frequent visitor during his tenure. Part of a high sheriff's role involves promoting the interests of the criminal justice system and supporting crime prevention initiatives. We would often see him sat in the audience watching our plays or some other event.

Before meeting George, the last time I was in the same room with a high sheriff was shortly before I was convicted of murder. I never did understand why some lady wearing a feathered hat and a traditional dress entered the court, interacted with the judge and disappeared again. But it did, for some reason, deepen my sense that something ominous was about to happen.

On this occasion, a high sheriff's presence was to distinguish both Aaron and me for our contributory, rather than felonious, deeds. George awarded us each a certificate for our services to the people of Suffolk.

Donations of artwork, which came from both the prisoners and the Suffolk community, were raffled or auctioned at these events and raised thousands of pounds for worthy causes. At one such event, where I was supervising a raffle, among the many prizes was a wide-angle, aerial shot of a mountain range somewhere in Scotland. Someone had donated this stunning image and everybody wanted it.

'George! Take a look at this,' I said, beckoning him over. I picked up the image. 'What would you like to put on that?'

'My God,' he replied. 'I have a little holiday home right on the edge of that mountain.' He pointed. 'Right there.'

After George finished telling me about his family outings at this very spot, he put in an offer on the image. Needless to say, he outbid everyone.

Since we were hoping to educate as well as entertain our audience, Max and I wanted to integrate as many historical facts into the play as possible. We figured that the best way to accomplish that would be to create a role for the King of England. We could then refer to the war with Europe's other great powers and the politics involved in issuing a letter of marque, a licence for pirates to steal from England's enemies. However, to our delight, we found that the monarch at the time our play was set was in fact female: Queen Anne. A short while later, trailers for *The Favourite*, a film about Queen Anne, flickered across the TV screen, which was a happy coincidence.

But we still didn't have enough actors for some of the other major roles. At least not until Alex – a prisoner who randomly appeared on the landing one day – volunteered to play the part of Lieutenant Davies of the Royal Navy. Alex had never acted before but he would soon learn. In a small room on the wing, Alex must have felt like Max and I had drilled him through an army assault course several hundred times. The only thing missing was mud on his face. But by the time we performed the show, Alex had not only morphed into an eighteenth-century navy lieutenant, with the articulation to match, he turned out to be one of our star actors.

After Celia Leggett, a staff member who worked in the Offender Management Unit, stepped in to play the role of Queen Anne exceptionally well, there was just one more key role left to fill – Cornelius Isaac, a Royal Navy lieutenant turned pirate who was Devilfish's antagonist. Since Levi had rejected our advances, Max proposed the idea of playing both Devilfish and Isaac, switching characters and using all sorts of trickery to make it plausible. So determined was he to make the play work, Max had even proposed playing Queen Anne as well until Celia stepped up. But there was a problem with Max playing both Devilfish and Isaac. At some point in the storyline, the two characters were destined to fight each other. For several weeks Max and I tried different prisoners but we just couldn't get the commitment or the quality we needed. Without an actor for Isaac, the show was finished.

But egos are strange things. While we fought desperately to find an actor, we hid our desperation when in the presence of Levi and pretended we didn't need him. He must have read the piece of the script we'd left with him at some point as, in the end, he wandered into the multi-faith centre to accept his rightful place in the cast.

During the second Butler Law course, the Learning Together team had been planning another event that would celebrate its ongoing success and provide us with the opportunity to speak more publicly about our achievements so far. In February 2019, the legal commentator and journalist Joshua Rozenberg attended Warren Hill's law library to record a piece for the BBC Radio 4 series *Law in Action*. It was called 'Jailhouse Law'.

'What's your name?' asked Joshua, while holding a large microphone to my mouth.

'Steve Gallant.'

'Just your first name.'

'Steve.'

Apart from mumbling something about Parliamentary Sovereignty and my correspondence with a PhD student, I don't remember much about the experience. After I'd finished listening to others speak, including Jack, who eloquently described some of the benefits of collaboration between academics and prisoners, I imagined I'd done terribly and put it out of my mind. As it later turned out, my interview was selected for the final piece alongside Jack's, Aaron's and Levi's. Once again, our voices in that quiet corner of the prison system had reached a national audience.

Having learned a valuable lesson on *The Citizen* about packing the cast exclusively with men, we introduced a female pirate aboard *The Albatross*. She was played by a prison healthcare nurse, a young lady whose shyness meant we had to either alter the composition of the next scene or do away with it altogether.

'She won't look me in the eye,' complained Levi as he stormed out of the room during one rehearsal.

It was a problem, but since this young woman had volunteered to help us we could hardly insist she gaze into the soul of a convicted murderer.

A few days later, we came up with a solution – a treasure chest built by one of the cast members who worked in the wood shop. Positioned in the centre of the stage, it allowed both characters to sit against it while facing slightly away from each other. It was the only way to get them comfortably on stage together but strangely it worked.

After Levi, Max and I had spent many nights working on the choreography for their swordfight, a scene that saw Isaac depose Devilfish to become the new captain of *The Albatross*, we showed it to our fight director during a practice session. Crouching on the floor and staring in amazement, he remarked, 'There's nothing more I can do to that.'

We were now creating our own fully functioning fight scenes, a skill that was put to dramatic effect in a final showdown that involved almost the entire cast. With the thunderous boom of cannon and musket fire blasting from the speakers, four Royal Navy officers charged from the back of the audience towards the stage, where the crew of *The Albatross* were waiting with their swords drawn. The governor and a few audience members even had to duck for cover during our climactic battle scene.

After we'd disappeared behind the stage, an out-of-breath fellow actor said to me, 'That was the best day I've ever had in prison!'

During one of our Learning Together sessions, Jack and Amy brought in a recent court ruling for us to scrutinise. The case related to the constructive dismissal of Nick Hardwick, the head of the Parole Board, by Michael Gauke, the then Justice Secretary. Stripped to its bones, the judge ruled that Gauke's interference breached the principle of judicial independence enshrined in the Act of Settlement 1701, a piece of legislation that prevented the monarch from interfering in the appointment of judges. Once again, we had stumbled upon a particularly apt moment in the timescale of history and linked it to an experience that we, the prisoners, were all too familiar with.

After the Royal Navy officers managed to overpower and arrest the surviving pirates, they were transported back to England to face their fate. With Isaac and Van Hepper on trial, the judge, played by Max, concluded proceedings with a guilty verdict for both defendants and a sentence befitting the period:

'Mr Isaac, only God knows what kind of mischief and mayhem you and that ghastly crew would have caused had the valiant Lieutenant-commander Davies not so courageously engaged The Albatross.

'Mr Van Hepper, you undoubtedly thought you could invent your own rules. However, the fact remains, following the Act of Settlement 1701, even Her Majesty the Queen of England no longer has divine authority to overrule the law. At least not all law.

'Cornelius Isaac, Jon Van Hepper, I hereby sentence you both to death by hanging. You will be taken to Execution Dock on the River Thames where, at low tide, each of you will be suspended by the neck, until life and breath have left your bodies.

'May God have mercy on your souls. Take them down.'

A gavel strikes. 'CRACK!'

It was truly remarkable to witness the collaboration between prisoners, staff and civilians during the production of these performances, about thirty cast and crew members in total. The enthusiasm was contagious and for us prisoners, it was the ultimate escape. Throughout the preparation for the performance, people would come to my cell and offer to get involved, sensing the buzz around our activities or seeing an opportunity to take a break from the monotony of prison life. The amount of hidden talent there was residing in minds of men who had, in many instances, made terrible mistakes in life never ceased to amaze me. Working on the play also gave me a greater understanding of human nature, particularly how some of the most challenging and complex members of our cast were also our most talented actors and writers.

And so we came to the climax of the play, in front of an audience containing our mentor Jack, who had done so much to help furnish the production with historical context. My character, Jon Van Hepper, was summoned to the stage, where, in exchange for the Spanish Corpora, my life was to be spared. The Queen of England had used her royal prerogative to grant me a pardon. Little did I know then just how prescient that scene would prove to be.

CHAPTER 23

Hope

In the UK, we are extremely fond of locking people up: we have the highest rate of incarceration in Western Europe. On the one hand, prison can function as a deterrent and help prisoners to get on the straight and narrow; on the other, it can desensitise prisoners to authority and prison conditions – or alienate them from society. Some people are too dangerous to be on the streets, so if imprisonment is the only realistic solution to keeping the public safe then it's justified. People have a right to be and feel safe.

But what is it that sustains public safety once someone has been through the prison system and made it to the other end? In my opinion, it's not so much the restrictions you impose while they are on licence or on day release, it's how you treat them prior to and while they are going through that process. Apart from the obvious things like employment-based training, education and offending behaviour work, encouraging desistance comes from treating prisoners with compassion and respecting what few rights they have.

On the whole, humans respond more positively to kindness, particularly when they, in the case of prisoners, have made substantial efforts to change. So as much as we need to deter people from committing offences, it's just as important that we encourage self-generated compliance, something that can be stimulated and sustained by treating people humanely and in the spirit of fairness and justice.

It was my experiences at Warren Hill that showed me the importance of compassion on the journey of change. Its model of imprisonment shone a light onto what is possible once you have a prison environment that is safe, settled and well managed. The Progression Regime may appear 'soft' – an uncomfortable notion for some in the context of crime and punishment – but when you compare it to the harm being caused by the violence and division at other prisons, a manifestation of an underfunded and less engaged system, it's clear which type of regime produces the best outcomes for society. Not every prisoner bought into the Progression Regime. And nor did every staff member – or manager, for that matter. The us–and–them mentality which holds back a large portion of the prison system is deep-rooted in the culture of the institution. But when it came to preparing men for reintegration into society, Warren Hill was in a league of its own. Despite holding some of the most dangerous prisoners, on paper, Warren Hill had the lowest recall rate compared to any other prison, a result undoubtedly assisted by greater resources, which kept the regime afloat, and its leadership, which allowed it to successfully navigate uncharted waters.

And yet, as invaluable as resources, good leadership and compassion are in being able to foster a sense of hope, that vital ingredient for change, I also came to learn that they cannot alone win the hearts and minds of everyone. When it comes to indeterminate-sentence prisoners, who are reliant on the Parole Board for release, the law, which is mostly seen as a tool to punish, remains another crucial component of hope.

On occasions, I witnessed decent prisoners detach from decent leadership and the prison community when the law had been poorly administered: Aaron's disappointment and subsequent withdrawal when he had done everything in his power to reduce the tariff on his sentence was the most glaring example. Fair laws and their proper administration reassure prisoners that if they engage positively and proactively with their sentence, their endeavours will be properly recognised – that they will be awarded their freedom and treated with dignity. Hope is not just something you can provide by offering opportunities to evidence change; it is manifested in the legal guarantees once change has been evidenced.

Making it harder for certain prisoners to progress through the system or achieve release, even when their change is corroborated, has become a major political focus over recent years. Alongside the benchmarking project that led to the redundancy of thousands of experienced staff, Chris Grayling slashed the legal aid budget by around 17.5 per cent. This gave him the pretext to remove funding for legal assistance for indeterminate-sentence prisoners at different stages of their sentence, like pre-tariff parole hearings (the point at which the Parole Board decide whether someone is suitable for transfer to an open prison). With access to legal aid withheld, untold numbers of ISPs were left having to navigate the complex parole process without a lawyer. For those who had their applications for release rejected because they had no legal representation, it was like receiving extra time for nothing, as some would have to wait years just to return to the same stage.

Following a lengthy judicial review brought by The Howard League for Penal Reform and the Prisoners' Advice Service, legal aid for pre-tariff parole hearings was eventually restored. The UK Court of Appeal ruled that Grayling's actions were unlawful.

Making it harder for indeterminate-sentence prisoners to progress through the system or achieve their freedom accomplishes nothing in terms of public safety, especially when the mechanisms for capturing risk already exist. Only the politicians benefit, as they can accumulate easy votes by claiming to be at the vanguard of public protection while judges who use poor reasoning or 'foreign' laws stand dangerously in their way.

But not all unwarranted laws are so definitively abolished. Although the IPP sentence was revoked by Parliament in 2012, it was not done so retrospectively. This caused little concern at the time, as it was assumed that the Parole Board would consider the existing IPP cases more sympathetically when they applied for their freedom. But that never happened.

As the years drifted past, the adverse effects of that political sidestep have been dreadful. One youth who was sentenced to four and a half months for a minor offence was still in prison almost a decade and a half later, and could, in theory, remain in prison for the rest of his life. With thousands still being detained (some under recall) by a law branded 'a stain on the justice system', it's little wonder that over a period of less than fourteen years, sixty-five IPP prisoners took their own lives. Throw into the mix all those prisoners who are convicted under joint enterprise, the law that allows someone to be sent to prison for the rest of their life for simply being in the wrong place at the wrong time, and the spaces that should be filled with hope, that vital ingredient for change and reconciliation, are, for some prisoners, filled with misery, resentment, violence and suicidal thoughts.

Prison is not meant to be pleasant and the challenges prisoners come up against there can assist greatly with change, as they did for me. But it shouldn't be a challenge to the point that it irreversibly damages someone's mental health or alienates them from society. Prisons should be places where those incarcerated are able to come to terms with their crime and move forward without hindrance once they have reduced their risk levels and demonstrated change. Using just a stick while omitting the carrot only hardens resistance and slows down progress. Many of those who find themselves in prison will have become the way they are because of injustice and unfairness throughout their lives, so to subject them to the same experiences only risks entrenching their problems and creating more distance between them and society's norms.

I'm not arguing for a soft approach for those who have committed serious crimes; I'm highlighting the counter-productive consequences that can occur when someone on the road to change is hindered for no good reason. I have witnessed the manifestations of many politically motivated policies or arbitrary measures over the years, but one of the most damaging effects is almost never spoken about: in the minds of those who rest at its sharp end, their conception of the law is not strengthened, it is weakened. And when that happens, society loses far more than it gains. As soon as people realise the law is not protecting them fairly, or their detention is arbitrary, it demotivates them until they become detached and end up dismissing the law on a more fundamental level. They don't break the law because it no longer exists to them. They invent their own.

On 2 May 2019, the multi-faith centre again filled up to celebrate the students' work at the end of the second Learning Together course. The guests included John

Samuels QC; David Ormrod, the Law Commissioner; Andrea Coomber, the Director of Justice; Simon Davis, the president of the Law Society, who'd sourced the funds for the Butler Law course, and Lord Hughes of Ombersley, former Justice of the Supreme Court.

The main purpose of the conference was for the students to present their completed legal advice guides and share their learning experiences with the guests, but Max and I had spied an opportunity. Still hyped up over the success of *The Albatross*, we decided to perform a scene from the play. There was no stage to hide behind and the multi-faith centre was flooded with daylight, full of prisoners, law students and all manner of professionals unsure of what to expect from these two funny-looking geezers. It was tense but thankfully we didn't miss a beat. Levi followed up with a powerful poem and we set the day rolling.

As well as a chance to show off, there was another reason for performing that scene: a message, expressed quite deliberately in the final exchange between the two characters in a prison cell, one a pirate, the other a Royal Navy officer. When Max's character complained that a life of folly 'would only make matters worse', I replied, 'How much worse can it get? You played by the rules but look where it got you. Sometimes, you have to invent your own.'

Without a doubt, everyone present at that conference was there because they believed in justice and fairness for all, but it's not every day you get to say what you want in front of a Supreme Court judge, let alone reveal a truth that remains hidden deep inside the minds of certain prisoners who have mentally detached themselves from authority. That's the beauty of art: you can push the boundaries while neither harming your audience nor yourself. The other truth was that not all those who were trapped inside the prison system across the country had a voice to express what injustice can do to the human mind. For those of us who can speak out, it is our duty to do so.

Although I doubt very much that our message fundamentally altered Lord Hughes of Ombersley's views on the application law, it was very kind of him to attend and he did acknowledge *The Albatross* in his own speech.

The conference was also a good opportunity for us to pay tribute to another, more satisfying truth. Thanks to our Learning Together friends, we had just experienced the most stimulating and inspirational two years of our sentences. They had provided us with a platform so we could share our insights and experiences with the wider Learning Together community and beyond, and so it was only right that we expressed our gratitude and appreciation for their contributions to our lives. Later that afternoon, Ryan and I delivered a speech to let Ruth, Amy and Jack know what they meant to us and thanked them for altering our perspectives on the law, life and the better-educated, and showing us compassion: *'When someone connects with you on a human level and shows interest in you as a person, regardless of your crime, this increases your self-worth, a vital ingredient for building hope. And where hope resides, so does the ability to envisage a better life beyond prison.'*

Whatever negative impacts certain aspects of the justice system were having on the rehabilitation of prisoners, in this small part of the system Learning Together, with support from Warren Hill's leadership and the Prison Service, made up for it.

★

With my pre-tariff parole hearing due in July 2019 and my sentence targets of further reducing my risk level and proving myself in cat C conditions complete, the prospect of moving to an open prison was firmly on the horizon. So, with just a few months left on the Suffolk coast, I had the chance to reflect on some of my creative experiences at Warren Hill and spend time with friends who, once I departed, I would likely never see again. When you spend years under the same roof, it's fair to say you get to know each other. It's also fair to say that while I've met some of the most dangerous people I've ever encountered in prisons, I've equally met some of the best and brightest. Prison is not what it seems until you experience it.

While the prison provided the space for art exhibitions, music events, performing arts and many other activities, it was us prisoners who used these to the best of our abilities, showing what can happen when a regime with resources offers a degree of autonomy to prisoners. But it was Aaron who brought magic to the prison.

Through the medium of performing arts, we explored the effects of law, politics and punishment on our lives in prison. We challenged ourselves, our peers and even the mindsets of some staff and managers. Sometimes we made great leaps forward and felt elated as our knowledge broadened, while at other times we felt uncomfortable when our long-held views about our fellow prisoners were challenged.

Some of us were unable to comprehend that the issue at stake was not the ideas we were proposing, but their core beliefs, culture or personal values that were holding them hostage to one perspective. But it didn't matter about the accuracy of our ideas, what mattered was that we were empowered to creatively challenge the forces that underpin the status quo, whether that was on the prison landings or in society's norms around how criminals ought to be treated. No one came away from those experiences without feeling the benefit and, I would argue, without being better prepared for the free world.

As for *The Albatross*, the performance had been recorded by a staff member, and Max and I had planned to enter it into a competition run by Koestler Arts, a prison arts charity. But the idea was killed off when we learned that Koestler forbid full-face video footage of serving prisoners, which is likely linked to prison rules. The concern was that the media might get hold of it and it would end up in the public domain. Instead, we entered a copy of the script into the contest and eventually received an award from Koestler. A short while later, ten chapters of *The Albatross* were used for a rehearsed reading at the Royal Court Theatre in London.

I had not yet reached the mountain summit but I'd achieved far more than I'd ever imagined I would at this stage of my sentence. Freedom was getting closer and the principle of perseverance my grandma had taught me as a child was finally paying off. But I wouldn't get to thank her in person, or even say goodbye. A few weeks before my parole hearing, news came through that she had passed away – cancer the cause.

My grandma had visited me when I was on remand in Hull prison, where, despite all evidence to the contrary, she'd said to me, 'You're innocent!' That was grandma – always on our side. My mum brought her up to visit me on one occasion in Gartree as well. Grandma was old and frail by then – she somehow seemed smaller than she had before. I was years into my sentence by then and it was a reminder once again of life continuing outside prison while it seemed to stand still inside. And now, a life I'd held dear had stopped outside, while I remained in prison.

'How are you?' asked Jack after he'd come to find me in the library. 'Ryan told me about your grandma.'

'Gutted. But I'm OK,' I replied. 'She lived to a good age.'

'If you need anything, just give me a shout.'

'Thanks, I'll be back next week.'

That was Jack, there whenever he felt people might need him.

My parole hearing, which had just one panel member, was relatively straightforward, thanks in part to Chelsea Turner, a prison law specialist.

'Are you sure you couldn't write properly before coming to prison?' asked the chair, sceptically.

I took it as a compliment.

My hearing lasted just over an hour and I received my answer the next day – category D status, meaning I could now transfer to an open prison where I would get the chance to venture out into the free world and begin to taste normality again.

It wasn't long after my parole decision that a letter from Learning Together arrived through the post. It contained an invitation to their five-year celebration and alumni event at Fishmongers' Hall, London Bridge. It seemed like it was going to be special day in the heart of London. Except I wouldn't be able to make it. Warren Hill had been waiting to transfer me to Britannia House in Norfolk, a 42-bed mansion that offered swift access to ROTLs (release on temporary licence). Provided I passed the relevant security checks, I would be able to leave the prison on day release not long after arriving. But it had a 50-mile travel limit that made it extremely unlikely I would be authorised to travel to London. So I put the idea of Fishmongers' Hall out of my mind.

But as the weeks began to pass, it became apparent that Britannia House was dragging its feet with my application. With no guarantee that I could get there within a reasonable timeframe, I made a snap decision to transfer to another open prison, HMP Spring Hill in Buckinghamshire. After saying the usual goodbyes to all, on 3 October 2019, I departed the walls and razor-wire fences for what I hoped would be the final time.

PART VI

The End of the Road

CHAPTER 24

Fishmongers' Hall

Approaching HMP Spring Hill, I was offered visual confirmation of the progress I'd made during my time in prison. Instead of the forbidding gate of Frankland, the prison at Spring Hill was open, and very leafy and calm. I could see the huts where the prisoners lived and the Big House, a nineteenth-century hall which served as a main office for the prison managers who headed up the different departments. And then there was the wildlife. Squirrels scurried quickly over the grounds and red kites circled gracefully overhead. The red kite had been reintroduced to Britain during the nineties, the numbers of this beautiful bird growing during my sentence. It was yet another reminder of the passage of time: while I'd been rehabilitating, an entire species of bird had been repopulating the countryside.

I could feel the difference at reception, too, where the staff were friendly and there wasn't that very concrete divide between staff and prisoner. While this certainly wasn't freedom, it was a big step in the right direction.

It was still prison, of course. The huts we lived in were a bit like chalets at Butlins but they certainly weren't the kind of place you'd choose to holiday in: freezing cold in winter and unbearably hot in summer, each of these huts was home to about twenty of us.

For the first time in my sentence, I shared a cell with someone. I'd been fortunate always to have had a single cell and I imagined it might be quite tricky to move into the cell of someone you didn't know. Thankfully, though, I got chatting to someone who arrived at the prison at the same time as me and we managed to get a cell together. Because I was doing a university course, I was able to move to a single room within a few weeks, which allowed me to better focus on my studies.

At Spring Hill, lifers are required to complete four visits to a local town, the first two accompanied by prison officer, before being allowed to venture away from the prison. But given that Fishmongers' Hall was just inside the 50-mile radius from HMP Spring Hill, it was too tempting not to at least try my luck.

As I anticipated, my application was rejected by a governor who informed me that there wasn't a staff member available for the escort.

'Unfortunately, I won't be able to attend,' I explained to Amy after setting up an email account. 'Hopefully, next year will bring more opportunities . . .'

'How frustrating,' Amy messaged back. 'Is there anything I can do? Don't want to undermine/get involved if unhelpful.'

'Of course, if you have any ideas. I'm not certain what can be achieved but you're welcome to,' I responded.

The next day, I was waiting in the dinner queue when an officer approached me.

'I'll be taking you to London next week,' he said.

Against all odds, my first taste of freedom in fourteen and a half years was going to be spent at an event right in the centre of London.

★

'Isn't this where the terrorist attack happened?' I remarked to Adam, my escorting officer, as we jumped out of the van on London Bridge. It was just after eleven o'clock on the morning of 29 November 2019, and this was my first taste of freedom in years. I'd recognised the peculiar-shaped bollards erected there following a terrorist attack two years earlier.

'Yeah, I think it is,' replied Adam as we walked along the bridge.

Even though it was dwarfed by the adjacent office blocks, Fishmongers' Hall still looked majestic. Facing the water on the edge of the River Thames, the grade II-listed building radiated history and opulence.

'Just enjoy yourself,' I whispered to myself as I walked up a short set of stone steps to the entrance at the side of the building.

Inside the foyer there were two doors that led into a hallway, a huge space with stairs that doubled off in opposite directions. Gold furnishings decorated the interior and the surrounding walls were adorned with historical portraits. Like a museum, rare artefacts and ornamental pieces embellished the place. I noticed a pair of narwhal tusks fastened to a wall, the relics of bygone fishing trips to the frozen north.

Simon Larmour, the PhD student who I'd met at Warren Hill, was near the bottom of the stairway, greeting the guests with a smile while handing out lanyards. It was great to see him outside the prison environment. At the top of the stairway, we were greeted warmly by John Samuels, who was standing at the entrance to a function room full of guests. Amy, Ruth and Jack briefly popped over to say hello and gave me a hug before racing off to finalise their preparations.

'This is Adam,' I'd say, to make sure my escort felt as welcome as I did. I recognised many faces, some from photos I'd seen at other Learning Together events. But many I didn't, including an Asian man standing near a window.

John beckoned me over to join him for some fish pie before the event got under way. We got chatting with the other guests while waitresses frequently breezed past with glasses of fresh juice on serving trays. When we'd set off that morning, it had been typically cold for late November, but not a cloud in the sky, and by midday the sun was shining brightly across London. Adam and I turned to look out of a tall window with a view over the Thames and London Bridge. Set among the other buildings on the far side of the river, the Shard glistened in the background.

'Wow, look at that,' we both commented, while Adam took a picture with his phone.

The contrast of these opulent surroundings with my usual place of residence was not lost on me. Nor was Learning Together's treatment of prisoners and ex-offenders. Their values never stopped blowing me away. If what they were offering wasn't enough to open your mind to a better way of life then nothing was. As for my first day out of prison, I could not have imagined anything more extraordinary. Before long, we filed into the banqueting hall to begin watching the event.

After Amy and Ruth gave a speech that summarised Learning Together's achievements over the previous five years, an American lady followed up with a talk on how simple derogatory words or phrases expressed to us in childhood can manifest negatively in later life. To the amusement of the guests, John Samuels volunteered an example of his grandmother calling him a 'silly boy' when he believed his behaviour had been worthy of praise. Then the Asian man I'd noticed earlier, who was now sitting near to us, contributed to the discussion. He explained that after he'd changed his mind about something important in his life, he told his friends that 'they were wrong' to continue thinking in the same old way.

I assumed he was an ex-offender or a prisoner like me. *Maybe he used to be part of a gang or had a group of friends who held antisocial views,* I thought.

Before I knew it, a couple of hours had drifted past and it was time for a short break. Simon came over.

'Jack has asked if you would like a photo with him,' he said.

I looked to Adam, who nodded.

Simon and I then went into another room. While someone took pictures of Jack, Ruth and me, David Ormrod, the Law Commissioner, jumped in and joined us in the photos. The mood was cheerful and it was nice to watch those who had helped me on my own journey enjoying the fruits of their labour. The atmosphere was filled with an exciting and optimistic feeling of 'what next?'.

It wasn't long before the event got under way again. While Jack went off to round up the stragglers, Ruth pulled me aside. A panel of guests, including Dr Jamie Bennet, head of operational security at the prison and probation services, was going to take questions on the importance of education in the journey to rehabilitation. My task was to read out a question, drafted by a serving prisoner, to the panel and summarise the response. I was a little anxious, because I wanted to get it right, yet excited as I returned to my seat in the banqueting hall.

Almost immediately after everyone had settled back down, a woman's high-pitched screams cut through the atmosphere. They were coming from downstairs. A guest made a joke, to nervous laughter. But the screams continued. The mood changed in the room. It sounded like it could be something serious. I wanted to investigate but any embroilment in what could have been an argument between two lovers may have led to a breach of my licence conditions. Given that it was my first day out of prison, I didn't want to make any hasty decisions. But still, the screams continued.

Adam looked at me. 'Stay there!' he instructed, before going to investigate.

I was itching to move.

Then Amy came rushing into the banqueting hall, pushing the door shut behind her while breathing heavily.

'Everyone stay where you are!' she ordered. 'It's Usman.' Amy began frantically dialling a number on her phone.

'Fuck this,' I said to myself. I jumped up and made my way to the door. As soon as I left the banqueting hall, I picked up my pace and made my way down the stairs. On the bottom few steps, a young woman was sprawled out on the floor with blood coming from her neck. Adam had his hand on her wound, trying to stem the flow. She was lifeless. Another girl, lying on the floor in the foetal position, had a large pool of blood forming underneath her. She looked unconscious – possibly even dead or dying. Other people, guests and employees of Fishmongers' Hall, were hidden behind curtains or cowering in corners.

As I reached the ground floor, I could see the Asian man I'd noticed earlier, through a doorway directly in front of me. He was inside the foyer, holding two large knives, one in each hand.

You must be Usman, I thought to myself.

Instinct took over. People were in trouble and there was a very real danger to all of us standing in front of me. I could not be sure of his next move but I wasn't going to wait to find out. The other guests remained vulnerable and these ladies needed medical attention – fast.

Usman turned to face me, his face expressionless. Right next to me on the carpet was a thick piece of wood that had been left there from clashes before I arrived. I picked it up and moved closer to Usman before launching it at his head with great speed. He ducked slightly and it missed by inches, hitting a large curtain behind him. Usman then moved towards me, pulled his jacket open and showed me an explosive belt strapped around his waist.

It looked real but, strangely, I wasn't fazed. If there was ever a fight worth having, even if it meant death, it was this one. Not for the love of violence but because his behaviour embodied the worst of humanity's creations. I wasn't about to fight Usman, who was in the midst of a terrorist attack; I was about to fight the manifestation of one of man's most desperate ideologies, one that had blinded him into thinking violence was the solution to life's problems.

Out of nowhere, a guy appeared next to me, holding out a narwhal tusk. I took it. Holding it like a lance in a jousting match, I entered the small foyer to fight Usman. My plan was to slow him down or stop him by any means possible.

There wasn't much room so I had to stay on my toes, light-footed. When Usman began to swing his knives towards me, I edged a little closer to him and managed to thrust the narwhal tusk into his chest. I hit him hard but, to my surprise, it seemed to bounce off, as if I'd hit something solid. Its limited effect made me hesitate – just for a split second. Then we continued to move backwards and forwards, jostling for better striking position. I struck out, missing by a whisker . . . His knives came close . . . and then, *Crunch!* I managed to hit him hard across the shoulder, snapping the narwhal tusk in the process.

Now unarmed, I backed off quickly as Usman came running towards me, swinging his knives. I managed to get back to the stairway. Usman stopped and returned to the foyer.

Get back in there. What's the matter with you? I said to myself.

I went back into the foyer and this time someone was standing at the other entrance, throwing whatever they could get their hands on towards Usman. I picked up a heavy wooden chair. As soon as Usman became briefly distracted, I raised the chair above my head and smashed it over his head and shoulders. Unarmed again, I backed away as Usman moved towards me.

'I'm waiting for the police! I'm waiting for the police!' he shouted, before suddenly pushing the foyer door shut to create a barrier between us.

He'd taken my blows well but I had a feeling that he was beginning to feel the heat.

I was so focused on Usman that I'd barely noticed that several people had congregated behind me. One of them grabbed the door handle to hold it shut.

'Don't let him rest,' I told him. Behind Usman was a side door with a security guard and several women hiding behind it, so gifting him thinking time seemed foolish.

As I pulled the door open to go at him again, Usman made his way over to the side exit to Fishmongers' Hall. He tried to slash a porter in his way, then he burst through the door. The porter pushed it shut behind him, holding it fast. A collective sense of relief filled the air.

But that doorway led straight onto London Bridge, where people were going about their business and didn't have a clue what was about to hit them. I raced over.

'There are people out there! Let me out!' I shouted, pulling the door open to go after him.

The streets were busy, the traffic on the far side of the road almost at a standstill. Usman was heading towards London Bridge. I could see several women walking directly towards him, oblivious.

'Get back!' I shouted, while waving my arms to draw their attention. 'It's a terrorist!'

Alerted to the danger, they turned and swiftly backed away. Other guests followed me out of Fishmongers' Hall and began shouting too.

Usman then came back towards me. Unarmed and cornered, I re-entered the building. The door locked shut behind me, preventing him from following me as he tried to reopen it. Then he set off towards London Bridge again. I picked up the broken narwhal tusk from our earlier clash and went after him.

As soon as I hit the pavement, Usman turned to face me once again. I struck him with the narwhal tusk but somehow he managed to grab it and rip it from my hands. I backed off towards the steps as he threw it at me.

I felt something cold hit my arm. It was the spray from a fire extinguisher directed haphazardly towards Usman from another pursuer. Usman turned and started running towards London Bridge. The man who'd handed me the narwhal tusk was now carrying his own and he chased after him along with the guy with fire extinguisher. I followed suit.

As we reached Usman, now on London Bridge itself, he turned to face us. Realising he was not going to shake us off, he lunged and began swinging his knives towards us.

Just grab him, I told myself. *Take him to the ground.* As my eyes tried to adjust to the low autumn sunlight slanting across London Bridge, I made a grab for his jacket with both hands. Finally, he was down and we had control.

'Grab his hands,' I shouted to the other two.

The chap with the narwhal tusk jumped in to take hold of Usman. Passers-by, who must have needed a moment or two to process exactly what on earth was going on, came over to help us. Some people jumped out of their cars to assist. One of the guests from Fishmongers' Hall came running up.

'Give him a kicking!' he screamed.

'No! Don't hit him!' I shouted back.

We had to retain control. He still held his knives and could detonate his explosives. And then, somehow, just as it appeared we had him under control, Usman managed to get back to his feet. Leaning my weight against him, I could tell he had a solid base, intensifying his threat.

Things moved fast in the melee that followed. We battled for supremacy. Then a gap opened for a moment, offering me an unobstructed view of his face. I punched him hard in the jaw. Crack! And another: Crack! This time, when he went down under us all, he remained there.

Moments later, unmarked cars carrying armed police officers screeched to a halt. Within seconds, they were leaping over the barriers with their guns drawn. Usman was now on his back, facing the heavens; his face remained expressionless, as it had been throughout.

While I still had hold of the scruff of his neck, I told myself, *He's finished.*

'Move! Fucking move!' the officers ordered. People began to disperse, leaving me and the chap who had the narwhal tusk in control of Usman.

'Bomb!' one of the officers shouted. 'Fucking move!'

I let go of Usman but the other chap still clung to him. I patted him on his back, tugged at his shirt and tried to get him to move. He didn't respond so I backed off out of the way. By the time I turned around, the chap was no longer there and Usman was being shot at – twice. To my surprise, he attempted to sit up and climb to his feet, which reinforced my original thought that he might have taken something to enhance his strength. Then Usman was hit with a taser to his head and shot again in the back, sinking him back to the floor, where he remained.

As I headed back to Fishmongers', it suddenly hit me.

'There are injured people in there,' I shouted to an armed officer while pointing towards Fishmongers'. 'They need help! Fucking hurry up!'

Back inside the building, the damage was horrific. Furniture lay strewn across the bloodstained marble floor. The physical carnage was mirrored in the people present: they were in shock, hysterical, devastated.

Armed officers burst into the building shouting, 'Armed police! Armed police – get down!'

I dropped to my knees on the stairs while they executed their manoeuvres. A couple of metres away, the young woman who'd been stabbed on the stairs remained motionless while paramedics tried to revive her. Alongside the guy with the tusk, I watched as they removed the defibrillator pads and shook their heads. Her name was Saskia Jones, a kind-hearted young woman who'd had a bright future in front of her. Adam remained seated next to her, head bowed.

After hearing a third burst of gunshots in the background, it suddenly dawned on me that I hadn't seen Jack. I approached Simon and asked if he'd seen him. Simon was in pieces. He shook his head.

'What, are you saying you haven't seen him, or have you?' I probed.

Simon continued to shake his head.

'Is he hurt?'

He was unable to speak or describe what he'd seen; I took it that Jack had been caught up in the incident before I'd arrived. I walked off to try and find out more but no one seemed capable of communicating. The shock factor of extreme violence was in full effect.

As we congregated in a function room, the chap with the narwhal tusk came up to me and shook my hand.

'My name's Darryn Frost. I work for the Ministry of Justice,' he explained. 'You saved people's lives.'

'That was my first act of violence in fourteen and a half years,' I said. I explained the vow I had made to turn my back on violence and how I had now broken this vow.

Even in the face of all this chaos and the unfolding emotional impact, for some reason I could not escape the fact that I'd just engaged in physical violence, that thing I had resisted so firmly over the years. This incident had driven me, pushed my instinctive triggers unlike anything had since my last offence.

But at least this time it was justified.

As we were escorted to a secure location, I learned that in fact Usman's explosive belt was a fake. It was convincing enough for the armed police to shoot him dead, of course, but I wondered how things would have played out had the explosives been genuine. Would more people have perished? Would I still be alive? Once again, I found my mind following the threads of what might have been – but it didn't bear thinking about. He'd done more than enough damage as it was – but we'd thankfully been able to stop him before he'd done any more.

Before being taken back to Spring Hill, I asked the police to try to keep my identity low key. The last thing I needed was every nutter in the prison system learning about my involvement. But I might as well have not bothered. By the time I returned to Spring Hill, everyone was talking about London Bridge and my involvement in 'taking down a terrorist'.

The next day, I remained in my cell and tried to process the events while various prisoners came by throughout the day to ask me what had happened – though some of them had more information than I did about the incident. I learned that the other woman who'd been stabbed multiple times by Usman had survived her injuries – just. But tragically, Jack Merritt, the young man whom I'd come to know through his extraordinary work in the field of justice, and the person who cared more for Usman's future than any of his so-called brothers, became his second fatality.

CHAPTER 25

The Royal Prerogative of Mercy

What made the terrorist incident that much crueller for the victims was that it was committed during their efforts to assist Usman with his reintegration into society. For their desire to help others, understand human motivations and provide insights that could benefit society, the victims paid the ultimate price. Having been welcomed so warmly into the Learning Together community, I could not fathom how Usman could betray the very people who wanted to help him. I really felt let down by the experience, devastated at the needless loss of life – and my sympathies went out to the families and the Learning Together survivors.

But it was predictable that not everyone watching from the sidelines was going to be so sympathetic. The incident played right into the hands of those who would rather see criminals hanged, drawn and quartered, and it was just a matter of time before the political repercussions kicked in.

Sure enough, with a general election under way, that's exactly what happened. To the fury of Jack's father, Prime Minister Boris Johnson used the incident as the rationale for sentence increases for violent criminals if the Conservatives were to be re-elected. Sending more people to prison for longer was the opposite of what Jack had always argued for. Following a landslide victory at the polls, Boris Johnson earned the right to continue as prime minister on 13 December 2019.

So while the Queen and Boris Johnson praised members of the public for risking their lives on London Bridge, those serving sentences for violent crimes were again about to feel the brunt. And so, ironically, was I.

In the aftermath of the attack, back at Spring Hill, I wasn't myself – I'd been knocked sideways by the incident. I never got to know Jack outside his professional life but I felt myself grieving for my mentor who had brought such light to my recent time inside.

Jack and Saskia Jones, two young people with so much to offer, so much to give, cruelly snuffed out in their prime, and for what?

On top of all this, it had been my first step outside of prison for almost fifteen years. That alone would have been a lot to process but to find myself using violence in such unprecedented circumstances had overloaded me and left me burnt out. It was a heavy comedown I was undergoing as I struggled to digest what had happened.

But I had to remain alert. My name had been circulating on social media and it was inevitable that my identity would soon hit the national news. Karl Turner, the MP for Kingston upon Hull East, who'd helped my family on several occasions, had got wind of my presence on London Bridge and wanted to assist me. On 19 December 2019, his friend, Neil Hudgell, a successful businessman and lawyer who owned Hull Kingston Rovers, a Super League rugby club, came to visit me at Spring Hill. A Hull lad himself, Neil remembered my offence from the local press in 2005.

After I'd summarised my journey since entering prison, Neil offered to help with press relations once my identity became public knowledge. We agreed that the only positive aspect of the London Bridge incident – the prevention of further injury or death – had the potential to be obscured by my conviction if it was left to the media to control the narrative. And that wasn't the only issue to consider.

One serving prisoner, James Ford, had already had his head hastily lifted above the parapet after someone had informed a newspaper that he was at the scene assisting the injured. A day or so later, it was beaten back down again. His victim's family were understandably troubled over him being called a hero in the press. If his experience showed one thing, it was that we had to tread carefully.

I was also aware of how sensitive the Ministry of Justice and Prison Service headquarters were to public scrutiny. Any adverse attention resulting from a press release could have serious ramifications. That Prison Service headquarters had barred me from attending Jack's funeral, even though Jack's family had reserved a seat for me, left me in no doubt about this potential.

So Neil and I had a minefield to cross, but I was confident that if I stayed within the rules, remained as sensitive as possible and gained the broadest possible support, I'd be OK.

After careful consideration of the prison rules that govern media contact for prisoners, Neil and I decided to prepare a press statement. The rules stated that there was no obligation for the prisoner to seek a governor's permission for media contact, but given the level of interest it would attract, it was only courteous to do so.

A couple of days later, I found myself at a prison manager's office at the Big House, the large Hall situated opposite the front gates of Spring Hill. The manager remained staring at his computer screen in the corner of his office, while sitting at a large wooden desk in the centre of the room was Spring Hill's chief governor, Becky Hayward.

'Take a seat, Steven,' she said.

'Thank you,' I replied.

'How are you feeling?'

'I'm OK, thanks.'

She pushed the order of service for Jack's funeral across the desk towards me: 'I thought you might like a copy of this.'

I took the booklet.

'It was a good turnout,' she said.

'I'm thinking of releasing a statement to the press,' I announced.

The Governor's face dropped; the manager averted his eyes from his screen.

'I haven't made my mind up yet but I would like your support if I did.'

'I'd prefer you not to,' replied the Governor in the sternest voice she could muster. 'But it's not within my power to stop you.'

'Look, for once we have a positive story,' I said, in the belief they might want to join hands. 'Let's use it as an example. Let's show that change is possible.'

'You won't alter the public's mind, Steven. People have their views on crime and punishment and that won't change.'

Realising I was not going to get their support, I left the office feeling deflated.

★

Back in my cell, I looked through the order of service, giving me a brief but powerful glimpse into Jack's life. Even in that slim booklet his character shone through. It made me feel the loss even more keenly. Not for the first time, I wondered what Jack would have thought of my situation.

A few days later, I received a follow-up message through the Big House manager: 'The Governor and HQ said it would be inappropriate to release a statement.'

The mood had clearly hardened. If I had thought that saving lives, many of whom were their colleagues, might have been just enough to convince them to take a more supportive approach, I was greatly mistaken. Despite media contact being perfectly legal, I was worried that speaking out would risk my freedom. I felt the idea slipping away from me.

'It's not looking good, Neil,' I confirmed over the phone.

'*Inappropriate*,' he replied. 'It's just an opinion.'

From a legal perspective, Neil was right, but legalities don't mean shit in prisons. A culture of ignorance and disdain for prisoners' few legal rights makes certain of that. No doubt the Prison Service leadership was pleased that lives had been saved and Usman stopped, but it was clear to me that they'd rather it had not been by a prisoner. It felt like I'd been patted on the back, put under the bed and told to keep quiet.

'Fuck them, Steve. They're only covering their own arses,' said Alan, a friend of mine. 'You didn't distinguish between yourself and them when you were risking your life, so why do it now?'

'You know what they're like, Alan. They'll get me back.'

'What can they do? You're not doing anything wrong.'

Even my assigned prison officer said to me, 'What are you worried about? I can't see anything wrong with it.'

And there I was, almost caving to the pressure of an elite group who disregarded the basic rights and protections of those under their care. I needed to snap out of it. What happened at Fishmongers' Hall was horrendous and heart-wrenching, but on that day, I witnessed something I'd never seen before. No one gave a second thought to status. Nobody said, 'Sorry, you're a prisoner, you shouldn't be involved.' And nor did I consider any civilian as undeserving of my assistance. Why would I? Academics, employees, civil servants, prisoners, civilians, students, ex-offenders and the emergency services all worked together to try to save lives and prevent Usman from hurting more people. So why should status only be irrelevant during the course of such a gruesome incident?

If the Prison Service and their Ministry of Justice overlords didn't want to use my story as a positive example of change, one that could contradict the prevailing narrative that prisoners are irredeemable and inspire their colleagues to see that their efforts are worthwhile, then I would. Too many positive stories had gone untold because of professional timidity or institutional prejudice, and that approach to public relations has distorted the nation's perception of prisoners and the prison system. The sense that something wasn't right ignited a spark within me.

'Neil,' I said. 'Let's do it. But if we're going to take the initiative, we need the broadest possible support.'

By now, the identities of all the other people who'd been involved at different points of the incident with Usman were in the public domain. Lukasz Koczocik, who'd been seriously injured, had fought Usman on his own before I arrived. And the chap who'd sprayed Usman in the face with a fire extinguisher was called John Crilly.

But there was another, a man who might well have saved me from being killed or seriously injured when I was facing Usman unarmed. Darryn Frost, a civil servant who worked in communications at the Ministry of Justice, had just released his own statement to the press. Although Darryn and I lived on opposite sides of the criminal justice fence, we joined hands that day in a shared endeavour to serve our fellow human beings, a moment symbolised when he handed me the narwhal tusk.

Neil made contact with Darryn, who offered feedback on my statement and then ran it past the Ministry of Justice news desk, who returned it with some editorial suggestions. We now had the necessary support. But we needed to move swiftly. Someone from the BBC had informed Karl Turner that they were planning to run a piece on my involvement.

Neil and I settled on a date but, before giving the final go-ahead, I had just one more thing to do. The press would undoubtedly reprint historical features related to my conviction, so I contacted Humberside Probation Services and asked them to notify the victim liaison officer about my statement's imminent release. It's the VLO's responsibility to liaise with victims and/or their families and forewarn them of significant developments. Given that Jack and Saskia's parents could also stumble across an article featuring images of their children, I arranged for them to be alerted too. A few days later, on 7 January 2020, my involvement in subduing Usman became national news.

As I expected, my offence was highlighted but the reporting was overwhelmingly positive. And most commentators were pleased to hear that I had not only saved lives but turned my life around. The same morning I was due to go out on my first local town visit, so I walked down to the dinner hall to collect my breakfast, feeling upbeat. It was a feeling that wouldn't last.

'Steve,' called an officer, 'I've been told to tell you, you're not going out.'

Thirty minutes later I was knocking on a Big House manager's door. On the large wooden table was a copy of the *Daily Mail*, open on a double-page spread recounting my statement and other aspects of the Fishmongers' Hall attack.

'Look at it!' they cried while pointing towards the pages. 'Look at it!'

'What?' I replied. 'What's wrong with it?'

'It's disgusting. You only did it for PR!'

'It's just a statement. Why are you so offended?'

'What about the kids?'

'What kids?'

'If the press turns up, what if the kids are out playing on the street?'

So absorbed in a moment of revulsion, this person had forgotten we were inside a prison.

'You're prejudiced, that's your problem,' I said calmly.

He stormed off. 'I have a meeting to attend.'

In hindsight, I should at least have let a governor know about the statement's imminent release. At least then they could have been better prepared for it and I might not have had to face the 'appropriate action' deemed necessary because of my 'transgression'. In fact, such was the seriousness of the non-existent rule I'd broken, by lunchtime I was being handcuffed and marched by several officers to the category B prison next door, HMP Grendon, to await my punishment.

Walking through the long, miserable corridors of Grendon, it was like jumping back in time: I felt like I was back on remand at Hull prison. Each step I had taken through my sentence had been a step forward, never backwards, and here, for doing nothing more than exercising my right to free speech, my journey had suddenly taken a sinister turn. A depressing feeling spilled over me.

When you arrive at a category B prison like Grendon, you're strip-searched. It's a far more intensive process than at the category D prison I'd thought was home, and all my thoughts and anxieties from my times in high-security prisons came flooding back to me. I thought I'd put all that behind me.

'I've spoken to Karl,' said Neil, after a flurry of phone calls. 'He's jumping up and down. Want us to make a noise about it?'

'If the press turn up outside the prison, they'll never let me back,' I cautioned. 'Let's stay calm, it shouldn't be forever.'

'OK, I'll get Karl to make a few calls, see what we can do.'

Later that evening, I was taken to an office.

'I've just come to see how you are,' said Governor Hayward, with a slight edginess about her. 'I've no idea why you're here.'

'Me neither,' I replied.

'I've just arrived back at the prison and not had the chance to speak to anyone.'

I had a sense that Karl's efforts had borne a positive reaction. But I remained calm and respectful. I never thought badly of Governor Hayward. She led from the back and was a stickler for the rules, but she seemed well-meaning.

'I just want to get back on track with my sentence, Becky.'

'I'll need to see why you were brought over here before I can make any decisions,' she explained. 'You're like a hot potato, Steven!'

I returned to my new cell on one of Grendon's therapeutic wings. But I remained depressed. The gloomy ambience created by the low ceilings, thick concrete walls, rattling pipework and the odd lifeless soul shuffling about was intensified by the fact that I was the only prisoner on a landing full of empty cells. It felt like I was in a morgue. For the first time in my life, a suicidal thought flashed across my mind.

I'd taken a huge step backwards. *What on earth has happened to my progress?* I asked myself. At that moment, I just couldn't visualise any sort of future, I couldn't begin to imagine it – and it filled me with depression. And then I began to contemplate a world without me in it. *Would that be the answer?* I asked myself. *Would that ultimately be the way out of this?*

I felt that I'd done something good and somehow been punished for it: I'd been made to take a massive backwards step in my journey to freedom, back to a closed prison, the last place on earth I wanted to be. I knew how the prison system worked: the slow and cumbersome bureaucracy meant that it was incredibly fast and easy to take a step backwards, but taking the same step forward was tortuously hard and slow work. I'd been fighting for fourteen and a half years to get to the position I was in now. Was I going to have to go through the process again?

If I was suffering from any trauma related to the terrorist incident, being returned to closed conditions only brought it to the surface. I lay awake most of the night, thinking about how my future would map out under the influence of people who were completely detached from those under their care.

By noon the following day, word suddenly came that I was able to return to Spring Hill, and two officers came to collect me. Something seemed to have changed for the better, a feeling that only increased as I walked the short distance back to the open prison.

One of the officers whispered under his breath, 'That was wrong, that. Should never have been moved. You deserve a medal.'

Back on open camp, the same vibe persisted as prisoners approached me to shake my hand. 'Fucking out of order that, mate.'

Then Alan shouted from his cell window: 'Hey, you were on TV earlier, getting praised by Bojo!'

What I didn't know was that while I was tucked away in Grendon feeling sorry for myself, fifty miles away in the Houses of Parliament, Karl Turner MP had risen to his feet to invite the prime minister, Boris Johnson, to 'congratulate and pay tribute' to me for saving lives. In an unprecedented moment for a Conservative PM, Boris Johnson replied, 'I think the whole House would agree, I am lost in admiration for the bravery of Steven Gallant and indeed others who went to the assistance of members of the public on that day and fought a very determined terrorist . . . my hope is that that gallantry will, in due course, be recognised in the proper way.'

If I was at my lowest point that morning, by that after-noon, after listening to those words on a recording played by my mother though a prison payphone, I was at my highest in nearly fifteen years. After returning to my room, I unpacked my belongings and crashed back on my bed to absorb the day's events. I had to give it to Karl Turner. He stepped up to support me and my family that day, and I'll always be grateful for that.

Things were suddenly back on track. By late January 2020, I was approved day release by Governor Hayward to study at Oxford Brookes University to complete my degree in business management. Finally, I was able to begin the last stage of my sentence, the chance to reintroduce myself to society and regain a sense of what it's like to be a free man again.

Throughout this time, John Samuels had remained in touch. He'd been fortunate. Had Usman made a beeline for him shortly after he began his attack, he would have stood little chance. Following the PM's remarks, the ground had been cleared for a tariff reduction and John had offered to assist me with the application process. Since 1997, only 27 life-sentence prisoners had received a tariff reduction on the grounds of exceptional circumstance. The court had previously relied on acts of bravery as a sound basis for a tariff reduction.

To assist with the application and the potential parole hearing, John recommended Lorna Hackett, a human rights lawyer. I'd met Lorna previously at a Learning Together event and was overjoyed when I found she was available to represent me. Lorna came with a great reputation and was highly regarded by many in the legal world.

There is quite a lengthy and intricate process to follow for any such application and this involves the Public Protection

Casework Section, a unit that sits within the Ministry of Justice and oversees the management of life-sentence prisoners. If the governor of the applicant's prison supports the application, the PPCS can then begin to collate any supporting documentation. Once the head of the PPCS approves the application, it will then be handed to the Secretary of State for Justice (at the time, Robert Buckland QC). However, even if a reduction in tariff is awarded, it can still take another ten months for the parole dossier to be collated and a parole hearing to be listed. Overall, the process can easily take 18 months. With just over two years left until my tariff expired, we were pushing it.

And then, just as Neil and I began the laborious task of gathering the relevant documentation, the whole world suddenly came to standstill. Covid-19 had been spreading like wildfire and, on 23 March 2020, the UK government imposed a national lockdown. With the pandemic inevitably set to consume already limited resources from a heavily bureaucratic system, the timing couldn't have been worse. But since we had nothing to lose, we decided to begin the process anyway. We felt a few months' delay would be reasonable, given the circumstances.

Yet, as that hot, boring summer gradually drifted past, and despite me having Governor Hayward's support for my application, by September 2020 the PPCS had barely wiped the dust from the paperwork. On gentle prodding from Neil Hudgell, an official from the PPCS tasked with processing the paperwork would only say that matters were still 'in hand' or that 'the application is still being considered'.

Unbeknown to me, an alternative route not only existed, it had already been alluded to during a conversation between Karl Turner and Boris Johnson during the summer. On

18 September, Karl Turner wrote a letter drafted by John Samuels and addressed it to Number 10 Downing Street on my behalf. Along with the relevant content, it included my wish to draw attention to the positive message it would send to prisoners across the prison estate if the application was successful. The letter concluded: 'Following our exchange in the House in January, you will recall speaking with me on leaving the Chamber and pledging to do all you can. Given your personal interest in Mr Gallant's case, I hope that you will honour that pledge.'

A week later, I was called down to the office of the Head of the Offender Management Unit. Expecting to receive negative news related to my request to get back out to the university, I was instead greeted with the news that I'd been given a royal prerogative of mercy and my 17-year tariff had been reduced by ten months. This meant I had the prospect of a parole hearing in nine months' time.

'Your parole process starts now,' explained the manager.

'Thank you, sir,' I replied with a smile, slightly taken aback.

'Oh, Steve,' called the manager as I headed towards the door. 'One more thing. I've been told to tell you not to tell anyone.'

'No problem,' I replied. 'I won't.'

I left the building and strolled back to my hut with the phrase 'royal prerogative' ringing between my ears; of course, I knew all about its historical significance from my time writing *The Albatross*. But I was full of mixed feelings. Given the loss endured at Fishmongers' Hall, it didn't feel like something to be celebrated. But its implications gradually become more significant to me as I went back to my living quarters. So much so that, on reaching my room, it struck me that I had no reason to keep such a rare honour to myself. On swiftly coming to my senses, I told everyone.

It would never have remained a secret, anyway. As a matter of fact, just a few days later, news of my sentence reduction was published in *The Times* newspaper. Though the article did contain a few inaccuracies: it omitted reference to the royal prerogative and mentioned that I'd killed a fireman. It turned out that someone from the Ministry of Justice had leaked this information to the newspaper.

A few weeks later, following a bit of snooping around by the good old British press, a more accurate account of the truth was revealed to the world. On 17 October 2020, the *Mirror* ran a front-page exclusive on my royal prerogative, a story that eventually circumnavigated the globe.

CHAPTER 26

Freedom?

With a potential parole hearing on the horizon and my university attendance re-established following the first lockdown, things felt like they were moving in the right direction once again. The advancement of my tariff expiry date had kickstarted a mechanism that invited the closer contribution of the National Probation Services (NPS). My parole dossier had been updated to help prepare me for life in the community. My behaviour spoke for itself. I'd educated myself to a high standard and achieved multiple awards, one of those for *The Albatross*. I'd completed every offending behaviour target set for me and my risk had been reduced to medium, a rarity for a lifer. I'd also been trusted enough to enter the community for twelve hours a day, six days a week, to attend university and local towns.

And now I had the offer of somewhere to live upon release. After striking up a friendship with Darryn Frost, he offered to support me with accommodation and employment. Darryn and I had also planned to set up a social enterprise and use our experiences to help prison leavers with their reintegration into society. There was nothing more I could do.

Upbeat and raring to go, I emailed my community offender manager the good news and my fresh intentions from the university, where I was in the final year of my business degree. Who could possibly view my record in a negative light now?

Enter Humberside Probation Services. Although they were tentatively supporting release, a Multi-Agency Public Protection Arrangements meeting had a different view of my conduct and plans. According to the board, whose opinions were recorded in my parole dossier, since I'd used 'violence against the terror perpetrator', they made a request for me to complete a psychological risk assessment, as well as a 'personality disorder formulation'. And since my friendship with Darryn Frost had been, according to them, 'forged in trauma', the idea that he could support me with accommodation on release was rejected. That the same dossier contained a prison psychologist's assessment that I presented no evidence of a personality disorder, nor had I been diagnosed with trauma, had clearly been ignored.

As I continued to flick through the pages of the dossier, I also came across other comments, probation updates which stated that my behaviour on London Bridge 'could be said to be reckless' and that I needed to look at my 'motivations and intentions'.

Despite the fact that I had not committed one act of violence since the crime that had resulted in my imprisonment, only reasonable force on London Bridge during extreme circumstances, these requests meant the Parole Board would now have several unticked boxes placed in front of them. A risk assessment can take many months to complete, and with Covid-19 restrictions preventing normal movements into the prison, it had the potential to delay my parole hearing.

And if that wasn't frustrating enough, Humberside Probation Services was planning to make a request to the Parole Board that, if they decided to release me, I should be subject to a bespoke licence condition which made it illegal for me 'to contact the press or respond with a statement without prior approval'. It was essentially a media gag. Beyond seven standard conditions applied to all licences, it's for the Parole Board to determine whether or not additional or bespoke conditions should be applied to someone's licence. The test is whether they are *reasonable* and *proportionate* in relation to an offender's risk. But the fact that HPS had even considered something so prohibitive, particularly as it had nothing to do with my risk, was concerning.

Along with my Spring Hill prison probation officer, I attended my first telephone conference with my community offender manager, Janine, who had not even interviewed me prior to writing up my parole dossier.

'You ignored an order from the governor not to publish your press statement,' she protested.

'I never ignored the governor.'

'That's what it says in your file.'

'My identity was about to enter the press, anyway. So what difference did it make?'

'You upset your victims, Mr Gallant.'

'But I contacted your department before I released the statement and asked your colleague to inform the victim liaison officer.'

There was silence . . .

'M . . . M . . . Mr Gallant . . .' she stuttered. There was more silence while Janine processed the implications. 'You murdered the victim!' she suddenly blurted out.

'You two, stop it!' interjected my prison probation officer.

Indeed I had taken someone's life and was rightly serving a sentence for it. But that wasn't the point. Nevertheless, the unrestrained desire to believe that I'd been non-compliant had gained so much traction with certain NPS professionals that they'd failed to realise it was them who'd faltered in their duty. And even though I'd highlighted this to Janine, she wouldn't acknowledge it, no doubt because it undermined HPS's request for a media gag.

But I had to tread carefully. Recall to prison is a straightforward process in the community, so if Janine's request succeeded and my access to media was in their hands, my freedom would become even more precarious.

As it turned out, it had been written in my file that I'd ignored the governor's orders. It was later removed, quietly. But the damage had already been done. Prisoners are entitled to communicate with the media; it's a fundamental right. But the MAPPA board were not focused on my rights; just the false belief that I had broken a rule was enough.

Yet Janine was blinded not only to the fact that she was dealing with a human being, but to the reality that was now about to unfold. She may have possessed an email address at justice.gov.uk, but I had some powerful weapons too. I had not broken any rules; I had remained sensitive throughout and I had obtained the broadest possible consensus for my press release. And I had one more weapon in my bag: my lawyer, Lorna Hackett.

In characteristic fashion, Lorna sliced through the board's crude misuse of power with surgical precision in her representations to the Member Case Assessment (MCA) team, the Parole Board officials who decide the preliminary merits of each case. In harmony with Lorna's reasoning, the MCA rebuffed the idea that a risk assessment or personality disorder formulation was necessary. Instead, they listed my case for a full oral hearing.

Meanwhile, the Public Protection Casework Section, whose role it is to pre-approve bespoke licence conditions, had vetoed the request for a media gag. It's possible Article 10 of the ECHR, the right to freedom of expression, saw to that. But HPS still proposed an amended version: 'to notify your offender manager in advance of any communication/statement to the press or engagement in media interview'. At first glance it seemed fairly innocuous, but this too could have had serious ramifications for me. At any moment, the media could say or print anything about me and I would have no way of proving that it wasn't me who imparted the information, putting my freedom at risk. We had to fight it, but without any evidence to prove I'd not broken any rules, there was a chance the parole panel would err on the side of caution and agree to the bespoke licence condition.

So I wrote to Governor Hayward about the adverse consequences I was experiencing due to my press statement. A week later, she wrote back confirming that I'd not ignored her order to communicate with the press and nor was it within her power to prevent me from doing so. Through a stroke of luck, I'd also managed to obtain the call log that proved I made the call to Humberside Probation Services, when I said I'd asked for the victim liaison officer to be notified. Suddenly, things were getting back on track again.

Shortly before my parole hearing, there was just one more task I had to conclude. I'd been summoned to attend the public inquest into the deaths of Saskia Jones, Jack Merritt and Usman Khan. It was being held at Guildhall in London, the venue chosen to accommodate the witnesses and professionals during the Covid-19 pandemic because the Old Bailey was considered too small to meet social distancing requirements. All the witnesses had been called to appear in person, but the Prison Service had informed the inquest organisers that my travel was too difficult due to Covid-19 and had arranged for my evidence to be provided via video link.

In response, I wrote a letter to the inquest judge, Mark Lucraft QC, to inform him that since I was currently travelling by train to a university in Oxford five days a week, travel was not an issue for me. I also expressed my hope that he, unlike the Prison Service, would not only treat me as a witness to those tragic events, but also as a victim.

A few days later, Judge Lucraft ordered my attendance in person.

At six o'clock in the morning on 21 April 2021, I was collected by three burly counter-terrorism officers and driven to London. From an underground carpark, they whisked me into Guildhall, where the inquest was being held.

'Take a look at this,' said one of the officers while beckoning me over and pointing into a huge cavern behind a large glass screen.

Tucked away under the building lay the ruins of a 2,000-year-old Roman colosseum. Like Guildhall itself, it was impressive. But just like at Fishmongers' Hall, it was another grand setting that conflicted with the tragic stories that were being retold in the great hall above, the most sobering coming from the victims' families.

Following their verdict that Jack and Saskia had been unlawfully killed, the inquest jury read out a statement criticising the agencies and people involved in the oversight of Usman Khan, drawing particular attention to a lack of information sharing and risk assessments conducted in the run-up to the Fishmongers' Hall event. Their conclusion and comments would ultimately lead to the demise of Learning Together.

After I'd finished my evidence, the detective chief inspector of Counter Terrorism Command shook my hand, thanked me for my evidence and offered me a reference for my up-and-coming parole hearing. After thanking him, I of course accepted.

Several weeks later, on 21 June 2021, after serving sixteen years and two months in prison, my opportunity to put forward my case for release had finally arrived. The parole panel was made up of three members, one of them a retired high court judge. They made it clear that if they decided to release me, the decision would be based only on whether I had met the test to be safely released into the community, not for what I did on London Bridge.

I wouldn't have wanted it any other way.

My prison probation officer, a lifelong employee of the Prison Service who knew me well, gave a fair and honest account of why she supported my release. As for Janine, she had an extremely narrow interpretation of what constitutes a reasonable and proportionate licence condition.

'It is for the Parole Board to decide licence conditions, not the MAPPA board,' barked the chair.

In the end, after Lorna had teased from Janine how she planned to use the media licence condition to restrict my freedom on release, her final request fizzled to nothing. Why? It wasn't only because of their inferior reasoning; it was because a faceless and detached group of public officials had failed to recognise that their requests were arbitrary and quite possibly in breach of my fundamental rights.

'What is your biggest fear, Mr Gallant?' asked a panel member.

I didn't hesitate. 'Returning to prison.'

'Have you thought about your actions on London Bridge and whether there were any similarities between those and your offence?' asked the same panel member.

'I have,' I responded. I described the contrasts in psychological terms – how my offence was motivated by a now defunct set of cognitive deficiencies layered over an unhealthy belief about violence, while London Bridge was more instinctive and selfless. And then I finished with a thought that not even the Ministry of Justice could deny or take away from me. I explained that after I'd seen those women seriously injured and had fought with Usman Khan as he tried to kill me, he had been laid on the floor, under my control, and someone had run up and shouted, 'Give him a kicking!' In that very moment, I had the choice to either use more violence on Usman or simply stand back while others set about him. But I did neither. Instead, I informed the panel, I shouted, 'No, don't hit him.'

'Thank you,' the chair went on to say. 'And good luck for the future.'

EPILOGUE:

The New Road Ahead

It is said that some of the greatest lessons in life can be found in some of the darkest places. I can attest to that. My greatest was that we are not, to varying degrees, as in control of our thinking and behaviour as we would like to think we are. Sometimes, you really don't have to be in a prison to be imprisoned, as I found out from personal experience.

One of my aspirations for writing this book was to open up the idea that violent crimes are not always committed with the clarity of mind that we sometimes think they are, nor as a result of some dark and unknown energy possessed or willed by the perpetrator. In other words, they are not exclusively born of evil, despite some violent crimes being the most horrifying and impossible to comprehend. It is far more complex than that, a fact I came to learn on the road to London Bridge, and one that was brought home to me again in a letter I received from a friend following the Fishmongers' Hall incident. He was still serving a 25-year sentence for murder:

Even when I didn't know that it was you who tried to fight off and stop that terrorist, I felt a sense of envy. I think you know what I mean. Envy because so many of us who have done such horrendous crimes as taking someone's life would love to turn the clock back and undo our wrong, but we cannot.

So we'd love a chance to prove that we are and can be good people. I am glad that you were able to do this. Of course, I wish that it never happened in the first place, such a horrible tragedy. But as it did happen, it also must be a good feeling that you were able to help stop more people getting hurt.

Who, with their faculties fully intact, would want to take another's life and condemn themselves to life imprisonment? And if a murderer is evil, why would they want to risk their own life to prove that they are good?

I'm not trying to justify violent crimes – my own crime or any crime, for that matter. I only want to contribute something constructive to a public debate that seems stuck in an archaic way of thinking in terms of how to deal with those who commit crime and how to keep people safe. Safety is a right and we all have a duty to help each other achieve that objective, but our national disinterest and antipathy towards anything remotely progressive, a gift to self-serving politicians and wealthy newspaper proprietors, has become a barrier to reducing crime. I can understand why the practice of being tough on criminals sits more comfortably with the public, but it just doesn't work.

There is great talent across the criminal justice system, as well as some very smart and inspirational governors, managers and staff who deserve enormous credit for keeping the Prison and Probation Service ship afloat during some of the toughest periods in its history. But they don't make strategic decisions and have little choice but to follow and implement policies that are devised by political advisers and senior civil servants who have a constant eye on certain sections of the media. Irrespective of the fact that some of their polices are counterproductive to the stated aims of the prison and probation services, many of today's poor results are born from the desire to keep politicians in power. Regrettably, the current state of politics in the UK means that they are more reliant than ever on political footballs. And few things in the history of politics is more convenient for accumulating votes than the issue of crime and punishment.

But there must always be hope, that crucial ingredient that kept me crawling along when deep in the bowels of the prison system. The events on London Bridge that day didn't just demonstrate the destructiveness of violence, they challenged a common thread that violence is inherent and therefore irredeemable in all individuals who use it. For sure, at least until we fully understand what motivates violence and certain risk-taking behaviours in each individual and can treat them accordingly, the ability to desist entirely will remain too challenging for some. But that is more a reason to work towards understanding it rather than throwing away the key.

In all its forms, violence is barbaric, but the main barrier to reducing it is public knowledge, a gap which could easily be filled by those with the means to inform. If that could be achieved, society can then engage in a more constructive debate about what our penal system should be doing, what its limitations are and what resources it should be provided with to appropriately meet its objectives.

Reaching my tariff expiry date was not inevitable, let alone reaching it successfully. Many indeterminate-sentence prisoners don't, and often for reasons beyond their control. But since I did, I would like to share some of the lessons I learned. They mostly involve developing a mindset once a problem has been acknowledged and some could, I would dare to say, just as easily apply to anyone who has not necessarily been to prison but has found themselves struggling in the depths of a self-induced furnace. Prisons, after all, come in different forms.

Despite my initial reticence, I took ownership of my actions. If it's someone else's fault, you can't heal and move forward. Pain, suffering, blaming other people, resisting change or the repercussions of your actions can all be part of the initial healing process. We've all made mistakes, been hurt and have good reason to complain, but if your actions are potentially hurting others or yourself, they must be overcome if you are to move forward in a constructive manner. To not do so, as I have witnessed throughout my sentence and in life in general, is to risk madness.

Taking ownership does not, by the way, mean accepting that people can treat you however they like. It's an internal process that is initially for your own sake, the positive outcome of which will become apparent to others in due course. It may also be that you are genuinely not entirely responsible for what happened. Even so, it's almost always possible to pinpoint a decision you made which led to you being in the wrong place at the wrong time. If not, it's still possible to own your situation, learn from it and improve the lot of others. No one on earth can begin to think about producing something positive for themselves or others while filled with hate, regret or self-loathing. Face your demons and use your situation or the negative energy of others to motivate you.

Never let your actions, other people or your situation define you. In the same way that I would never allow my actions at Fishmongers' Hall define me, refusing to define myself as a murderer was another factor that helped me to progress. This is not the same as refusing to take owner-ship of your actions. If you allow yourself to be defined by your past or given status, you place yourself in a box that leads you to think and behave in a rigid way. I saw this a lot in prison. A convicted armed robber lets everyone know he's an armed robber, and everyone treats him with a certain level of respect. He lives up to it. However, if the 'armed robber' has a sudden change of heart, any attempt to redefine himself can draw suspicion from his peers, potentially placing him at risk. The internal and external pressures to remain the person you have defined yourself as can override the desire to escape from the mentality that brought you to your predicament in the first place. In essence, you run the risk of perpetuating your own imprisonment. If you can avoid, at all costs, conforming to the expectation of your peers or certain sections of society without fearing you may lose something, you can gain everything.

There were times when I found my sentence challenging, especially in the early days when I was still confused as to how I had landed myself in such a terrible situation. But after I began to grasp the fundamentals and settle in, I realised something quite profound. Irrespective of the poor conditions engulfing many of our prisons and the impact that this can have on those residing within them, with the right mindset, they are still places where you can learn and grow. Significant limitations abound but it's still true that the chief agent among all the decision makers on how you live out your sentence is you. No matter where you are or what the conditions, take your sentence as the biggest opportunity you will ever have in your life to develop or reinvent yourself. Don't wish your sentence away. As far as we know, our time on this planet is extremely limited and we only get one go. If you can accept that each second you spend on this planet is precious, then so is each moment spent in a prison cell.

I'm not suggesting these things are easy in practice, but nothing worth its salt ever is. As my story has shown, even though my thinking and behaviour were deeply ingrained, once I had accepted that part of my world had been made up of self-defeating ideas, I was able to make a conscious effort to react less impulsively to the events around me, a decision which allowed me to walk among some of the most dangerous prisoners in the country without ever once having to lift a finger, either offensively or defensively, to achieve my objectives. It challenged me but it paid off because I accepted my lot, refused to conform to the expectations of others and used my time to better myself.

Having said that, I don't remain unburdened by my actions. As long as I reside on British soil, I will be subject to a life licence and therefore potential recall to prison for the rest of my life. But I accept that that's nothing compared to the price I bestowed upon my victim. While I can never truly give back in this repect, I hope that by sharing my experiences and insights, society might benefit in some way.

Of all the misfortunes I encountered through my journey, nothing has been as tragic as what happened to Saskia Jones and Jack Merritt, two amazing and talented individuals who were killed for nothing more than pursuing their dreams of helping others and improving social cohesion. The world is a lesser place without them.

Had the threat of terrorists and extremists leaving prisons been taken seriously when it was so obviously a looming security issue, then that tragedy could well have been avoided. Following the London Bridge attack, as well as a separate terrorist attack in Streatham, south London, at least the authorities were finally beginning to take some form of action to manage this ongoing threat to society. Both attacks were committed by men who'd been managed by the National Probation Services after being released on licence from British prisons. As a result, the National Security Division was set up to manage terrorist-related offenders in the community. Given the lack of resources across the NPS, it made perfect sense to create a specialist unit. It's just a pity that the impulse to manage the public's perception of all things justice again became the overriding priority. Shortly before my parole hearing, my case-file was transferred over to the new National Security Division.

'It's not because you've done anything wrong,' Janine reassured me. 'It's only to manage the media interest in your case.'

So, I was now going to be managed in the community on a par with terrorists by a division that was set up in reaction to an incident in which I had risked my own life to help others. And not only that: the NSD suddenly decided I was going to be held for six months in a bail hostel, which was unusual for a medium-risk prisoner like me. And all for PR management.

In keeping with this approach, on 27 July 2021, my official release date, the NSD applied to the Parole Board for a licence condition to allow the police to collect me from the prison so they could drive me 35 minutes to the bail hostel. For the privilege of a free taxi ride, I would have to remain in prison for a further seven days.

'What's the matter with you?' came the response when I raised my concerns. 'It's only a week!'

So out came the guns again: 'It should not be forgotten,' Lorna counterargued. 'Mr Gallant has had well over one hundred independent visits to Oxford, as well as a visit to the same hostel . . . It is unclear why this is being proposed now, on the day on which he should be released, rather than properly considered at the Parole Board hearing nearly five weeks ago.'

The Parole Board agreed and ruled that it was not reasonable or proportionate based on my risk to the public to have me collected by the police from the prison.

Once again, the judiciary put the arbitrary application of power from public officials back in its place. Though I still didn't get out on my official release date. The probation services made me wait the extra week.

I once shared a piece of my writing with Jack Merritt and he advised me that it's always best to finish on a positive. That handy little bit of advice, characteristic of Jack, has always remained with me.

On 3 August 2021, I said my final goodbyes to the men I'd been locked up with for the previous decade and a half and strolled down to the prison's reception with my belongings. Turning to face a backdrop I'd come to know so well, I thought about my long journey to get here, one that began in a dark and violent place but ended with Queen Elizabeth II's final signature for the rare gift of a royal prerogative of mercy.

On reaching HMP Spring Hill's open gates, I was greeted by Darryn Frost, who was waiting for me by his car. We smiled and shook hands, a little bit like that moment when the detective greeted me outside the police station, all those years ago, when I handed myself in. This time, with the sun shining on my back and a hard-earned degree